M000003458

# STRENGTH
# IN
# NUMBERS

## THE TEAM APPROACH TO
## BIBLICAL COUNSELING

## MARK E. SHAW

## STRENGTH IN NUMBERS

by Mark E. Shaw

Scripture references are quoted from
The English Standard Version of the Bible
and where noted,
The King James Version
and The New King James Version

Cover design by Melanie Schmidt

**ISBN 1-885904-72-X**

PRINTED IN THE UNITED STATES OF AMERICA
BY
FOCUS PUBLISHING
Bemidji, Minnesota

# TABLE OF CONTENTS

## Section 3: Implementing the Team Biblical Counseling Model

# INTRODUCTION

**I myself am satisfied about you, my brothers, that you yourselves are full of goodness, filled with all knowledge and able to instruct one another.**

Romans 15:14

The movement for biblical counseling seeks to reclaim the care of souls to their rightful owner, the Lord Jesus Christ. Here is a very brief case for biblical counseling as opposed to the two other types of counseling: purely secular counseling and "integrated" counseling. (I refer to the latter as a "mixture" approach because it attempts to "mix" Christ-centered truths with secular, man-centered ideas).

## Purely Secular Counseling

Think of a Christian you know who is really struggling with a serious problem such as pornography, adultery, stealing, drug addiction, depression, anxiety, or the like. To whom might you send them for "counseling" right now? The average Christian would likely send them to a local psychologist or psychiatrist depending upon the problem. If that psychologist is NOT a Christian, would he or she be likely to recommend prayer, Bible study, church attendance, or fellowship with other believers? The answer is "no."

So why do Christians turn to Christ on Sundays but turn to secular psychological "experts" for emotional problems in their soul on Monday through Saturday? Is the body of Christ unable to deal with serious problems like depression and anxiety? Are the Holy Spirit and God's Word inadequate to address these types of problems? If the answer is "yes," then why do we even go to church on Sundays? Why not worship at the psychologists' office instead?

Secular counseling offers some temporal help but no eternal hope to clients who may either be unbelievers or Christians. In a purely secular, psychological approach, counselors do not point their clients to Jesus Christ, the Savior, or to the truth of God's Word. There may be temporary benefits to a secular approach but without the Gospel, there are no *eternal* benefits.

The secular approach does not call sin "sin" and offers no answers for sin. Therefore, the secular approach replaces the descriptions of sinful thinking and behaving found in the pages of the Bible with man-centered labels, which excuse it. Secular counseling calls sinful thinking and behaving a *disease* or a *mental illness*, relieving a sinner of responsibility for his/her sin. And of course, there is no Christ offered for forgiveness of sins in this approach. In the temporary world, this approach offers minimal relief; however, in the eternal world awaiting all of us, this approach offers a destination of hell according to the Bible.

Secular psychology enthusiasts wrongly argue that they address "emotional" problems and not "spiritual" problems, but that's not true. Psychology means the "study of the soul." Psychologists analyze the "heart of man", meaning the inner man consisting of the thoughts, attitudes, and motives of man. These inner thoughts and attitudes lead to emotions and actions. Emotions cannot be separated from one's internal thoughts, attitudes, and motives which is why most "cognitive-behavior" therapists are marginally successful. They deal with the thoughts, attitudes, and motives that cause emotional problems.

What you may not realize is that your beliefs about Christ determine your attitudes, thoughts, and motives. If you believe Christ is your Creator, Owner, and Lord, then that will influence how you think and act. Emotions will also flow out of your thinking and acting. You will find joy in living for Him by serving others. However, if you do NOT believe that Christ is Lord, then you will not live for Him or for His glory. Instead, you will live for your own pleasures and glory. Your thoughts will be about how to please yourself and you will earnestly seek to do so. Your emotions will be perceived as positive when you are pleased and negative when you are not pleased. You will lead a life of instability and be a "double-minded" person (James 1:8).

Thinking and acting always produce emotions. Actors in Hollywood know this truth when they are required to play a death scene. Obviously, in real life, two actors involved in the death scene know that the actor is not really dying. In order to elicit the emotion required to play the part convincingly, the actors must *think* about a sad situation that occurred in real life (like the death of a loved one). When this happens, tears flow as emotions are produced convincingly.

## What It Means to Think Biblically

For this reason, it is vital for biblical counselors to address the person's thinking. Biblical thinking is a rarity in the life of many believers in Christ. One problem is that our language has changed. Many Christians are unfamiliar with biblical words. We know psychological words like "ego" and "narcissistic" but rarely use words like "pride" and "sin." It is an epidemic in our culture. The psychological terms and the biblical words are very similar in meaning except for one major difference. Biblical words like "sin" are strong and bring conviction because they put the responsibility for the behavior upon the person. Secular, psychological words like "narcissistic" often supply an excuse and shift the responsibility from the person behaving selfishly as a result of his or her "disease," upbringing, environment, or mental illness. These are very important, underlying ideas that shape our culture's thinking.

Christians must reclaim the language. We must replace secular, worldly labels and thinking with biblical terminology. Biblical words place the responsibility for wrong choices squarely upon the shoulders of the person doing the choosing. Biblical words call sin "sin" because there is a remedy for sin: the atoning work of the Lord Jesus Christ upon the cross at Calvary. To deal with these sin problems accurately and effectively, biblical counselors must reclaim the language.

Before Christians can reclaim the language, Christians must first learn to think and speak biblically themselves. You cannot give away what you do not possess yourself. You cannot speak, think, and behave like Christ without the truth of God's Word that reveals the character of Jesus and without the empowering of the Holy Spirit that indwells the believer. To be a Christian, one must have the Holy Spirit living inside of him so that he can properly interpret and apply the Bible in his life.

In a purely biblical approach, the truth is presented in love. Man is told that he is a sinner who has disobeyed God according to his own choices. The wrath of a just God will be poured out upon sinners in hell unless they repent and place their faith in the atoning blood of Jesus Christ upon the cross. This approach offers both a temporary benefit of forgiveness of the guilt of sin as well as an eternal benefit of everlasting life with God.

If biblical truth is never presented, the Holy Spirit has little to work with to bring conviction to a person desperately in need of real change. The Holy Spirit convicts us of our sins to bring us to repentance and faith in Christ. It is a good thing to be convicted of sin when we have offended a Holy and just God who punishes sin. The Good News is that Christ Jesus bore the punishment for the Christian's sins at Calvary and the wrath of God was satisfied. The justice of God was upheld by the sacrifice of Jesus.

## An "Integrated" Approach to Counseling

The second approach to counseling is the combination of man-centered psychological theories and Christ-centered, biblical principles which has been referred to as the "integrated" approach to counseling. While many well-intentioned Christians promote this approach, I strongly believe it is deceptively dangerous and has the potential of deadly consequences. Psychological counseling theories are dangerous because the majority of them are man-centered, not Christ-centered. Admittedly, psychological observations (called "descriptive psychology") may be useful information but caution is still advised.[1]

---

[1] For more on this subject, a good book to read is <u>Deceptive Diagnosis</u> by David Tyler and Kurt Grady. It is available through Focus Publishing (1-800-91-FO-CUS) and can be ordered online at www.focuspublishing.com, 502 Third Street NW, Bemidji, MN 56601

James 4:4-5 says: **"Do you not know that friendship with the world is enmity with God? Therefore whoever wishes to be a friend of the world makes himself an enemy of God."** The church has a "friendship with the world" in the realm of psychological counseling and it is called the "integrated approach." More and more churches are turning to the so-called "wisdom" of the world that often opposes the very Word of God in the arena of caring for people's souls. Psychology means "the study of the soul" but it carries out that study of the soul devoid of biblical truth. In fact, the majority of psychological constructs are in direct opposition to the Word of God.

Caring for souls has been stolen away from the church. Some Christians no longer go to the church first for help with "emotional" problems. Some Christians do not even turn to the church for "spiritual" problems. Where do Christians and unbelievers go for help and real answers to their emotional and spiritual problems? Do they go to psychological "experts" or to pastors, elders, deacons, or committed Christian friends? Many church leaders are no longer shepherding their congregation, and as a result, families are suffering.

In conclusion, biblical truths and man-centered ideas do not mix and will only lead to confusion for Christians. I think this integrated approach leads to weak, confused Christians who are more susceptible to the lies of Satan and this world's system. I am not attacking the well-meaning Christians who subscribe to this approach though I do believe they are misguided, just as I was only a few years ago until the Lord opened my eyes to see that the two could not be mixed. When I realized this, I began to grow in Christ as never before.  Praise the Lord!

**What is Biblical Counseling?**

Biblical counseling has been defined by one source as "a process in which a biblical counselor helps a counselee find and do God's will, thereby cooperating with God's plan to progressively conform the counselee to the image of His Son (progressive sanctification)."[2] This definition is solid and all that I would add is that biblical counseling is relational in the sense that the goal is to help reconcile unbelievers to God for the first time and to reconcile sinning believers back to God. "Repent and believe" is the simple phrase needed for sinful man whether he is an unbeliever who is yet to know God as Savior or he is a believer in Christ who has merely strayed away from living an obedient life unto God. Both persons must be reconciled to God; therefore, biblical counseling is a process whereby the counselor opens God's Word to the counselee for the purposing of leading the person to Christ.

A "mixture" approach of Christian principles and secular, psychological, and man-centered concepts often confuses a person who is seeking to know Christ. There is not always a clear presentation of the Gospel in this approach since man-centered ideas do not promote the need for a Savior caused by our sin. I worked in this field for several years and the people counseled are unstable and act as if they are riding a rollercoaster because they receive mixed messages that confound them. For this reason, I am now purely a biblical counselor though I am admittedly influenced by cultural, psychological ideas. None of us are immune to the influences around us but I believe that we must start and stay with the Holy Scriptures of God for good counsel and reject the lies of Satan and this world – just like Adam and Eve should have done in the Garden. Any psychological idea of man that causes doubt and does not agree with Scripture must be laid aside in favor of biblical counsel because rightly interpreted, the Bible is the Word of God and "the truth will set you free" (John 8:32).

## A Biblical Counseling Approach

As mentioned earlier, biblical counseling is grounded solely upon the Word of God and the Holy Spirit working through the biblical counselors. The most effective biblical counselors are those who have a strong relationship with Jesus Christ, know how to

2 Definition obtained from Biblical Counseling Association at this website www. biblical-counsel.org.

yield to His leading, and speak the truth of His Word lovingly to others. Biblical counselors are concerned for their counselees and speak the hard truth in order to warn them about the dangers of thinking and acting apart from God's will (which is called "sin").

Biblical counselors want to warn others that they are responsible for their choices and thoughts which may lead them to ruin. They provide hope in Christ when they teach counselees that sinful choices and thinking can be replaced with godly choices and thinking in accordance with the Word of God. They provide practical help from the Holy Scriptures, not personal opinions. Finally, biblical counselors point a counselee to the forgiveness in Christ available when the counselee repents of the sinful thinking and acting.

The benefits of being "Holy Spirit-led" by obeying the commands of God and walking in His paths of righteousness allow the Christian to experience life—not the spiritual death of sin's separating powers. Sin separates Christians from experiencing the intimacy and closeness of a healthy relationship with God and others. Sin causes one to be vulnerable to a variety of attacks from the enemy. Just as a physical virus such as HIV weakens the body making it vulnerable to common illnesses ultimately bringing death, sin is a spiritual virus that weakens your spiritual, inner person making you susceptible to satanic attacks that can kill you. Sinning is foolish as it only leads to death and destruction. In personal ministry, discipleship, and biblical counseling, sin must be addressed. Because of the justice of God, sin cannot be "winked at" and one cannot pretend it does not exist.

*Biblical counseling reclaims the care of souls to the body of Christ.* In many churches, members are merely satisfied with attending worship services and teaching times. While the Sunday morning preaching ministry is essential to the church today, a team biblical counseling ministry of the church is also vital. When properly taught, lay persons can work together in teams to provide biblical counseling to the body of Christ as an "in-reach" and "out-reach" ministry. It is an "in-reach" ministry in that it provides practical, biblical help to members of the church. It is an "out-reach" ministry in that it provides hope in an evangelistic format for those who are not yet members of the church. Why send people to unbelieving, psychological so-called "experts" when the church of Jesus Christ is capable and competent to provide biblical answers? Romans 15:14: **"I myself am satisfied about you, my brothers, that you yourselves are full of goodness, filled with all knowledge and able to instruct one another."** With proper training and instruction, lay persons in the church can become knowledgeable in the Word God, rightly apply it to emotional and spiritual problems, and instruct, counsel, and encourage fellow members of the church.

Though often neglected today, personal, "house to house" ministry was an important part of the life of the early church as seen in Acts 20:20: **"how I did not shrink from declaring to you anything that was profitable, and teaching you in public and from <u>house to house</u>"** (emphasis mine). The apostle Paul said that he taught "from house to house", teaching biblical principles privately in homes likely as a personal ministry similar to Christian, biblical counseling. Paul was one of the first Christian biblical counselors!

The church is to be on the offensive, leading the world, not following it. Many times the church buys into secular programs and tries to "Christianize" them. Such is the case in an "integrated" approach to Christian counseling that attempts to mix some of the unbiblical, man-centered ideas of psychology with biblical, God-centered ideas derived from the Word of God. The two are incompatible since the world attempts to push God out of their approach and the Bible centers upon Christ in everything.

## Team Biblical Counseling Defined

It has been difficult to communicate the concept of "team biblical counseling" to others for several reasons. First, many people are unaware of what biblical counseling is and that it exists as a discipline unto itself.[3] Second, I am aware of no other ministries or secular agencies that counsel in pairs for 90% of their sessions. (At times, we meet for one-on-one discipleship meetings but those are infrequent.) Our desire is to lead the world and biblical counseling into doing ministry in a modality that is more effective, balanced, safe, powerful, and loving. We believe that team biblical counseling will "catch on" as people begin to commit to a team philosophy of ministry.

At first, many of our biblical counselors expressed their reservations and concerns about the team approach, but now they are excited about it, and are convinced it is a powerful way to do the work of ministry for many reasons (as you will learn as you read further). Working in tandem has been a blessing to novices and more experienced counselors alike. The fruit of our ministry is not only being produced in the lives of our counselees, but in the lives of the counselors who are serving in pairs.

The biggest concern I hear now is about scheduling and the practicality of this model for ministry. While scheduling in teams can seem challenging, we have found that the Lord has allowed us to experience very few problems in that area. We assign each case to a primary counselor who has a partner in ministry. If that partner is unable to attend a session (since most of our biblical counselors are volunteering their time and conflicts do arise), then the primary counselor may have a different partner at the second session (or later sessions) but this has not been a problem to the counselees who have established a comfort level with their lead, primary counselor. The new counselor to the subsequent session usually peruses the P.D.I. (see Appendix A) beforehand and is aware of the presenting problems. Shortly into the session a new counselor often "jumps into the flow" of the session. It simply has not been problematic either from our standpoint or for the counselees we are privileged to serve.

---

3 The National Association of Nouthetic Counselors (NANC), the International Association of Biblical Counselors (IABC), and the Association of Biblical Counselors (ABC) are three national organizations that exist to promote biblical counseling in the United States.

In summary, team biblical counseling is new and unknown for the reasons stated above. My first hope is that you can now see the importance of a pure approach of biblical counseling over the other two philosophies of counseling. My second hope is that you are now open to exploring the rationale and implementation of at team ministry in this book, and that you will begin a team ministry approach of biblical counseling in your local church whether you are a pastor or lay biblical counselor. My final hope is that you will see how this type of team ministry can be utilized effectively in missions work around the world as we endeavor to fulfill the "Great Commission" of Matthew 28:18-20: **"And Jesus came and said to them, "All authority in heaven and on earth has been given to me. [19] Go therefore and make disciples of all nations, baptizing them in the name of the Father and of the Son and of the Holy Spirit, [20] teaching them to observe all that I have commanded you. And behold, I am with you always, to the end of the age."**

## Modeling Christ

In a fallen world cursed because of man's sin, there is no shortage of problems and hurting souls seeking real answers. As biblical counselors or lay ministers, we have an important duty to serve and represent our Lord. We know that the answers are found in Christ Jesus our Lord alone, and that the Bible reveals Him and His divine character to us in an intimate and personal way. We are called to share His love and salvation with others and help them to center their thoughts upon Him. Biblical counseling gives us an opportunity to do just that.

In biblical counseling, we help people to "think biblically." Thinking biblically means that one's thinking in the flesh is unbiblical. Thinking in the flesh apart from Christ is off-base and wrong. Truth does not come from within us. Absolute truth comes from God's Word alone. The Bible is our source of truth. The postmodern churches of today believe there is no absolute truth, leaving truth open to individual interpretation. The Holy Spirit enables us to understand biblical principles properly. It is the indwelling of the Holy Spirit that enables Christians to properly interpret God's Word and to do the work of ministry.[4]

The goal of ministry in a biblical counseling and discipleship context is to lovingly confront someone when their thinking is unbiblical. By "confronting," it is meant that someone is lovingly warned that wrong thinking is unbiblical and could lead to further problems. Warning someone that the bridge is out so they do not drive ahead and crash is a good thing. Often, counselees believe the lies of Satan or this world rather than the truth of God's Word. Other counselees believe that the passions, feelings, and desires of their flesh are to be obeyed rather than the commands given by the Word of God. These are the most frequent types of problems that counselees have and the remedy is the same: knowledge of God's Word through the illumination of the Holy Spirit and then obedient action to carry out God's Word through the power of the Holy Spirit. God's Word and the Holy Spirit are inseparable in biblical counseling, discipleship, and personal ministry of any kind.

Let's be biblical. Let's counsel others with the balance of compassion and doctrine. Let's present the truth of God's Word in the love of the Holy Spirit. Let's lead the world in the arena of helping people through counseling by conducting personal ministry in the safety, wisdom, and love of a team approach. Let's give the glory to Christ and submit to His leading.

One of my mentors used to say, "Biblical counseling is the best game in town," as there is no other approach that matches it. In secular counseling, there are over 250 psychological theories and most of them differ significantly from each other. In integrated Christian counseling, there are over 150 approaches. In biblical counseling, there is merely one approach with the authority and power to change lives and offer hope and help to hurting people. With the addition of teamwork and God's grace in biblical counseling, the "best game in town" just got better!

---

[4] Philippians 2:12-13.

## Summary

My passion is to get lay persons involved in ministry. When a fan watches a football game, the fan may scream, holler, and cheer for his team but he is merely a spectator who has no power or influence on the outcome of the game. Many Christians today are similar to a football fan as they merely sit in the stands watching others do the work of ministry. If you are a biblical counselor or a pastor already, then your task is to equip the saints for the work of ministry (Ephesians 4:12). In the following pages, you will find one safe, effective, and balanced vehicle to use in your local church to motivate your lay persons to become participants and not merely spectators. The task of shepherding the flock of God is daunting. In Exodus 18:14-18, Moses was exhausted by fulfilling his call to the ministry alone:

> "When Moses' father-in-law saw all that he was doing for the people, he said, "What is this that you are doing for the people? Why do you sit alone, and all the people stand around you from morning till evening?" [15] And Moses said to his father-in-law, "Because the people come to me to inquire of God; [16] when they have a dispute, they come to me and I decide between one person and another, and I make them know the statutes of God and his laws." [17] Moses' father-in-law said to him, "What you are doing is not good. [18] You and the people with you will certainly wear yourselves out, for the thing is too heavy for you. You are not able to do it alone."

There are so many Christians who need loving counseling and there is only one of you. Perhaps you have said, "I wish I could clone myself and help more people." Well, there is a way, and I think that after reading this book you may begin to see a sign of hope that will energize your ministry and empower others to use their gifts for building up of the body of Christ.

# SECTION 1

# NOURISHING
# THE
# BODY OF CHRIST

# Chapter 1

# THE POWER OF CHRIST

**His divine power has granted to us all things that pertain to life and godliness, through the knowledge of him who called us to his own glory and excellence, ⁴ by which he has granted to us his precious and very great promises, so that through them you may become partakers of the divine nature, having escaped from the corruption that is in the world because of sinful desire. ⁵ For this very reason, make every effort to supplement your faith with virtue, and virtue with knowledge, ⁶ and knowledge with self-control, and self-control with steadfastness, and steadfastness with godliness, ⁷ and godliness with brotherly affection, and brotherly affection with love. ⁸ For if these qualities are yours and are increasing, they keep you from being ineffective or unfruitful in the knowledge of our Lord Jesus Christ** (2 Peter 1:3-8).

Christ works through His body, the church,[5] to seek and save those who are lost. Christ also works through His body to build itself up in faith, grace, love, and truth (Ephesians 4:12 and 4:29; 1 Thessalonians 5:11; Jude 20). Satan and the promotion of the world's systems of lies will not build up. One of the means God uses to build up the Body of Christ is the "personal ministry" of biblical counseling.

Biblical counselors uniquely view God's Word of truth as sufficient and use it as a standard to address all types of problems. Problems that are labeled spiritual or emotional (i.e. fear, worry,

---

[5] The word, 'church' does not refer to a building but to a group of people called Christians.

anxiety, sadness, depression, anger, etc.) are commonly addressed by biblical counselors. Sin issues of the heart are primarily addressed since biblical counselors understand that thinking and behaving are important to God. He holds people responsible for how they think and act (Matthew 5:21-30). There is no problem too big for God and He has given us all we need in His Word (2 Peter 1:3; 2 Timothy 3:16-17). A biblical counselor is not called to give personal advice, but is called to point the counselee to specific passages of Scripture that address his/her problem.

One aspect of biblical counseling that sets it apart from all other types of counseling is that a biblical counselor relies solely upon the Holy Spirit to speak through him/her to the counselee. The Holy Spirit does the work of counseling because He works in the heart of the Christian counselee to bring insight and change. The Holy Spirit enables the counselee to rightly understand God's Word of truth and gives them the power to obey His Word in action. The Holy Spirit works in conjunction with God's Word. The two are inseparable. That is why secular counseling that fails to present God's Word of truth is ineffective.

Quite simply, the biblical counselor is called to speak the truth of God's Word in the love of the Holy Spirit to hurting souls. This can be done in a formal counseling session or informally when one Christian talks with another Christian. In 1 Thessalonians 5:14, the Lord calls all Christians to lovingly speak the truth to people we encounter: **"And we urge you, brothers, admonish the idle, encourage the fainthearted, help the weak, be patient with them all."**

*After much urging from a fellow church member, Edgar and Ann agreed to go for one last counseling session before their divorce was made final. They'd been to counseling before so they knew the routine. In the past two years, they'd been to a psychiatrist's office and a professing "Christian" counselor for marital problems. They were not sure what would be different this time, but were willing to commit "just for their friend."*

*Ann made the appointment and hurriedly filled out the paperwork. When they arrived at the first meeting, they really didn't know much about this particular counseling center other than it was located in a church and called itself "biblical." They were mildly surprised when not one counselor but two were present in the counseling office: a male and a female. "This is different," thought Edgar. "Are we so bad that we need two counselors?" thought Ann walking into the meeting room.*

*After the opening prayer and initial questions, Edgar is asked how he has contributed to the problems in their marriage. Ann is surprised that Edgar is so open about his own failures, especially with two counselors present. His willingness to be honest encourages Ann greatly as the session progresses. She has not remembered Edgar admitting his faults to her or anyone. There is a seriousness of purpose in the room, and this is strengthened with two counselors present. Ann also feels safe. Soon each confesses sins, asks forgiveness, and commits to plans of practical repentance in just the first session!*

*What Edgar and Ann do not know is that both of their counselors are simply members of that local church who were trained lay counselors in biblical counseling. Because the session is so Christ-centered and grounded in the Scriptures, neither Edgar nor Ann think to ask about the counselors' credentials (or lack thereof). They are later surprised to learn that their counselors are committed followers of Christ without formal training in psychological counseling. The only rigorous training these counselors received was in biblical counseling and team ministry.*

*As team ministers, Edgar and Ann's biblical counselors are much stronger and balanced in their approach. You see, each counselor is an extremist at heart. One counselor errs on the side of speaking the truth but not always with a loving attitude, while the other errs on the side of being "loving" without saying the "hard," truthful things that often need to be said. These shortcomings are nullified when the two of them work together in a team counseling setting. Edgar and Ann have no idea that this team dynamic is so important or will be so beneficial to their marriage. God in His wisdom and sovereignty has brought Edgar and Ann to a unique ministry that offers hope and biblical help to deal with the difficult issues of marriage and a looming divorce. By God's grace, they will stay committed to their marriage vows and honor Christ. They will learn how to biblically communicate, resolve conflicts, and speak the truth in love to each other. Edgar and Ann will continue to grow in Christ as they meet with the same two biblical counselors in future joint counseling sessions. In God's economy, the two biblical counselors are growing in Christ, also, by learning from their partner to become more balanced and Christ-like.[6]*

Biblical counseling is designed to motivate counselees to change in a manner that pleases God and produces holiness in their thinking and actions. The motivation to change is wrought by the indwelling of the Holy Spirit in the Christian counselee's heart. The Christian counselee hears God's Word, understands it rightly by the indwelling of the Holy Spirit, feels convicted about how his/her thinking and acting have not been pleasing to God, and then is empowered by the Holy Spirit to implement godly changes in thinking and in action. God gets the glory in purely biblical counseling because He is doing the work of counseling. The counselee is held responsible for his/her thoughts and actions, and God is working in their heart to bring about change. The counselee is called upon to trust Christ by being obedient to His Word of truth and to repent for any unbiblical thinking and acting.

---

[6] All the vignettes contained in this book (set off by italics) are complete fabrications.

## The Glory of God

The biblical counselor should not receive the praise and glory for the changes that occur in the counselee's heart. He or she is merely a conduit through whom the Holy Spirit works. Having worked alone for many years as a counselor in both the secular and biblical counseling arenas, I have observed that sometimes the environment of singular counseling encourages an unbiblical attitude whereby the counselee promotes the counselor to a level of "expert". They look to him/her for biblical wisdom; sometimes even elevating the counselor to the place Christ should have in their heart. Christians sometimes have a tendency to try and solve problems on their own, or ask others for help before they go to their heavenly Father in prayer, and by searching Scripture for biblical wisdom. Often, counselees are tempted to call their biblical counselor first, essentially omitting a consultation with God. I encourage people to cultivate their relationship with God and commune with Him through prayer and Bible study far more than they commune with their biblical counselor.

Only the Lord Jesus Christ is the "expert" and He has provided us with His Word of truth to reveal His thoughts, purposes, and plans for us. He has also provided all Christians with an indwelling of the Holy Spirit so they can rightly interpret His Word of truth and carry it out in power in their lives. Philippians 2:13 states: **"for it is God who works in you, both to will and to work for his good pleasure."** God merely wants a biblical counselor to point the counselee to Him so that the counselee will depend upon Him and no one else. Placing trust in anything or anyone other than Christ is sinful, even if the counselee is trusting in a biblical counselor.

As you go forward with biblical counseling, please heed this gentle warning about your approach to ministry and consider the environment of formal counseling that you may be creating for your counselees. You may be unaware that your counselees are beginning to "idolize" you rather than focus upon Christ. Despite your best efforts at explaining that you are not the source of wisdom, but that Christ is, and you are simply His messenger, the counselee may not comprehend the message you are sending. Here is one reason why:

The heart of man is inclined to idolatry. Idolatry is worshiping anything and anyone other than Christ. With the world's constant bombardment of messages that a "counselor is an expert," counselees are encouraged to view biblical counselors as "experts," too. In my opinion, we must do everything possible to point counselees to Jesus Christ, the real expert and the source of their joy and strength.

Being ministers of Christ, sometimes I think we erroneously try to be Christ to others, especially in the area of biblical counseling. Pride is a temptation for every servant of Christ, especially for those who work alone in counseling. We must remember that we are merely the conduit and He alone is the living water. He can use anyone who is submitted to Him and who has an understanding of His Word to be His water fountain. He does not "need us" yet He desires to use us for His own glory and for our own good. It truly is an honor to serve Christ in any capacity, anywhere, and to anyone.

Another danger of counseling alone is that *none* of us has the strength of the Lord Jesus Christ who walked the earth as fully God and fully man. Jesus knew the intents of the heart of man (Luke 9:47). As a man who ministered to others, Jesus had a decided advantage over us in His ministry because of His divine nature. He had a decided advantage over His disciples, too. Though they walked with Him and though we walk with Him, and He indwells us, we are not Him. We are simply ambassadors of Him and are called to lead people to Him, not to ourselves. Our ministry is about Him not us. We should never steal His glory! I am concerned that counseling alone sometimes inadvertently encourages "glory-stealing" from God, the rightful Owner of all glory and everything good.

There is something you can do to change this situational problem. You can begin counseling in teams of two. You can change the environment by simply adding another biblical counselor to your counseling sessions every time you meet with a counselee. It may seem like overkill at first, but I can tell you as someone who has firsthand experience in team counseling as well as solo counseling, the team approach to ministry is extraordinarily more powerful, effective, safe, and balanced. The team approach has revolutionized the way we do counseling in our ministry, and I will never seek to do counseling ministry alone again.

Jesus came to earth to save sinners and He calls us to make disciples as He did. He lived, walked, ate, cried, loved, and invested His time and energy in twelve men specifically. Except for prayer and giving His life upon the cross, Jesus rarely conducted the work of His ministry alone. He was a public figure even in private where His disciples watched Him speak the truth in love to others as well as to them! He was a consummate teacher and the perfect balance of grace and truth (John 1:17). He modeled that for His disciples and for those hurting souls to whom He ministered. You can do the same in this sense: whenever possible, never "do" the work of ministry alone again.

Whether you are going to the hospital to visit the sick or counseling someone in your local church, bring someone else with you to "do" the work of ministry as a team. Have the mind of Christ in the sense that you are always teaching someone else how to serve others when you are doing the actual work of your ministry. Somehow, our culture has become so segmented and individualized that we have lost the art of replication. In reality, we have lost the art of disciple-making because we think in terms of individual ministry and miss golden opportunities to teach others through teamwork and modeling and promoting practical experience for novices.

## Beyond the Counseling Room

One goal of this book is to challenge you to re-think the way you are "doing ministry." Although this book is written for the discipline of biblical counseling, it has wider applications than that one facet of ministry in the local church. Whether you are a pastor or a lay person, whether you are involved in formal or informal "counseling," whether you are male or female, and whether you are a biblical scholar or a novice, the principles in this book apply to you and the ministry the Lord has given you.

Not everyone is involved in *formal* ministry. However, every Christian is called to be involved in the ministry of sharing God's love to those who are lost and do not know Him as Savior. Christians are also called to speak the truth in love to fellow believers of Christ in order to build up the body of Christ. Informal ministry opportunities exist for all believers in the form of husband-wife relationships, parenting, encouraging friends, admonishing extended family members, relating to co-workers, and the like. We are all ministers of Christ.

The Christian life consists not only of educational learning in a classroom setting but of the actual practice of "doing the work of ministry." James 1:22 warns us: **"But be doers of the word, and not hearers only, deceiving yourselves."** If we sit in Sunday school classes, Bible study fellowships, and attend conferences for a variety of biblical topics but never actively apply those principles to our lives, then we are simply being "hearers" of the Word and failing to do what God has called us to do (Ephesians 2:10). A music theory student who takes many classes in music theory but never practices or plays an actual instrument is not a musician. Until he or she plays and practices the instrument, the music theory student remains a music theory student. God has called us to be musicians who get involved in ministering to others for the sake of His glory and for their good.

## Action Word

Sadly, my computer's spell check and dictionary program contains thousands of words, but it does not recognize the action word "discipling." The action of "discipling" others is an unfamiliar concept not only to my computer but also to most people in the world today—even to many professing Christians! Many Christians are neglecting the call to disciple others as the means of spiritual growth in the body of Christ.

Biblical discipleship has even become a lost concept in the home. Husbands neglect their call to teach their wives about the Word of God (1 Corinthians 14:35). Fathers are called specifically to disciple their children according Ephesians 6:4: **"Fathers, do not provoke your children to anger, but bring them up in the discipline and instruction of the Lord."** Many mothers are failing to teach their children about Christ and His Word. Are Christian parents actively raising their children to be disciples of Christ in their very own homes? Are Christians actively making disciples of Christ in their very own churches?

Most parents recognize that children model their parents' actions and words, whether for good or evil. Modeling, or discipleship, is one of the strongest means of spiritual growth because it involves action! Actions are more powerful than words. Discipleship by modeling is the way that Jesus taught His followers. It was His divine method of growing those often scared, faithless men into stalwarts of the faith. Jesus did not just preach a good sermon to His disciples and go home; instead, He preached sermons in word and in deed by living out obedience to God, and modeling the love of the heavenly Father before them. The disciples of Jesus Christ observed Him while He lived. Then when He ascended into heaven and the power of the Holy Sprit was sent to indwell them (Acts 2), they were able to put their learning into action.

If we could liken current ministry trends today to a spectator sport, such as basketball for instance, then we could say that too many Christians are on the bench or on the sidelines - just spectators, though they may be energetically cheering fans. Teamwork in ministry is a powerful way to get less experienced or anxious persons "involved in the game". My goal is to encourage lay persons who possess a solid theology (though not perfect), a surrendered heart to Christ, a willingness to serve Him for His glory and the good of others, and a working knowledge of the Bible to do the work of ministry because they are the body of Christ. One man does not a body of Christ make – so we should not elevate one man to a special status of "expert."

Discipling others is an action. One of the reasons that biblical counselors are not replicating themselves is that lay persons rarely are given opportunities to observe and then serve in this ministry. In some organizations, biblical counseling has become specialized and limited to those who have special training and seminary degrees. This must not be the trend in biblical counseling!

While I agree that biblical counselors must be skilled, knowledgeable in the Word of God, and sound theologically, I do not think that a grandmother who has raised her children in a godly manner, studied the Scriptures over the years, and has the indwelling of the Holy Spirit is incapable of counseling a younger, Christian woman. She is competent to counsel other women biblically[7] and would do a much better job than any unbelieving secular counselor who does not embrace biblical principles and only promotes man-centered ideas.

**Take Action**

Whether you are involved in formal ministry as a pastor or biblical counselor, or you find yourself with an informal ministry as a lay person who often gives advice to friends, here is my challenge as you begin doing team ministry. It can be challenging and inconvenient at times, but the benefits are well worth the effort. The apostle Paul demonstrated the power of Christ in word and deed as 1 Corinthians 4:20 affirms: **"For the kingdom of God does not consist in talk but in power."** I want to challenge you to never "do ministry" alone again whenever possible, and I submit to you that doing all ministry in teams is a much more realistic possibility than you may think. Be creative and intentional, looking for ways to incorporate a partner into your daily ministry life. Involve this

---

[7] A reference to Dr. Jay Adams' <u>Competent to Counsel</u> book.

person, too; they are not just an observer. In other words, allow them to participate and speak. Encourage them to take faith-filled risks and assure them that you will lovingly, gently correct their errors. Place confidence in the indwelling of the Holy Spirit who lives within them; He will bring to their remembrance the Holy Scriptures (John 14:26). Give them the grace to grow in Christ through the experience of conducting ministry with you but for God's glory.

When you begin to "do" team ministry, you will be pleasantly surprised with the results. Both the counselees you minister to and the biblical counselors involved in ministry grow exponentially in Christ in a team paradigm because they observe and experience firsthand the mighty power of Christ to change the human heart. Both the biblical counselors' hearts and the counselee's heart conform to the image of Christ and are transformed by the power and grace of God.

Romans 12:1-2 states: **"I appeal to you therefore, brothers, by the mercies of God, to present your bodies as a living sacrifice, holy and acceptable to God, which is your spiritual worship. Do not be conformed to this world, but be transformed by the renewal of your mind, that by testing you may discern what is the will of God, what is good and acceptable and perfect."** Christ is "in the business" of changing hearts by tearing down the lies of this world and Satan and replacing them with biblical truths that transform the Christian's thinking. When a Christian begins to think like God in accordance with His Word of truth, a Christian will then begin to act like God in ministry and accomplish His good, acceptable, and perfect will. Team ministry provides exceptional opportunities for mind renewal to occur by God's grace.

I urge you to pray about starting a biblical counseling ministry in your local church if there is not already one in existence. But you do not have to do it alone! The principles in this book are designed to help you to utilize a TEAM ministry approach embracing all the variety of spiritual gifts in the body of Christ. Lay persons can and should do the work of ministry according to Ephesians

4:12: "**to equip the saints for the work of ministry, for building up the body of Christ**." Ordained leaders, biblical counselors, and lay persons should be working together for the kingdom of God. A team approach to ministry offers balance, wisdom, safety, experience, truth, and love. It is a model that may be utilized in many different aspects of ministry. When you witness for yourself the power of Christ in the team approach to ministry, God might just change the way you think and "do" ministry forever.

Chapter 2

# THE IMPORTANCE OF DISCIPLESHIP

**And Jesus came and said to them, "All authority in heaven and on earth has been given to me. Go therefore and <u>make disciples</u> of all nations, baptizing them in the name of the Father and of the Son and of the Holy Spirit, <u>teaching them to observe</u> all that I have commanded you. And behold, I am with you always, to the end of the age"** (Matthew 28:18-20, emphasis mine).

### Malnourished Christians

The church today is very similar to the believers addressed in Hebrews 5:11-14, **"About this we have much to say, and it is hard to explain, since you have become dull of hearing. For though by this time you ought to be teachers, you need someone to teach you again the basic principles of the oracles of God. You need milk, not solid food, for everyone who lives on milk is unskilled in the word of righteousness, since he is a child. But solid food is for the mature, for those who have their powers of discernment trained by constant practice to distinguish good from evil."** Reflect upon your own spiritual growth in Christ for a moment. Who were the people who had an impact upon your growth? Whether we realize it or not, we need others to nurture us spiritually as a mother physically nurtures her newborn baby. Christ works through His people to build up His children.

How did your spiritual growth occur? You may have been part of a small group, or maybe one person led you to our Lord Jesus Christ and gave you some teaching about the Christian faith. Along your spiritual journey, you may have had other mentors teach you more about Christ. Not every Christian has had the opportunity to have a mentor to disciple them. Unless you were in that small minority of Christians who had a spiritual mentor, you were very likely on your own in the early days of your Christian faith. You were saved and then left alone with minimal instruction in the lifelong process of sanctification. Your growth in Christ occurred slowly, if at all.

If you had a mentor or "discipler," then you were enormously blessed by God. This shouldn't be so rare! As a baby Christian, you were in danger of being led astray. Think about some of the mistakes you could have avoided and how much more rapidly you would have grown in your faith if you'd had a mentor to shepherd you. Unfortunately, we are seeing many believers leave the church today, and one factor is the lack of true discipleship and intimate relationships with more mature believers immediately following conversion.

Just as a neglected newborn baby needs nourishment, the Christian church today has a lot of spiritually malnourished "born again" Christians. Are we failing to emphasize spiritual growth in Christ through personal mentoring relationships structured for the discipleship of newborn Christians? How can new Christians discern what is good spiritual food and what is poisonous doctrine? They cannot any more than newborn babies are able to detect the nutritional value of the milk offered to them. The newborn baby simply craves that milk with passion and will drink anything to satisfy a hungry appetite.

One very effective way that this problem of malnourishment in the body of Christ can be addressed is by having your church embrace the "team" concept of ministry. A sermon preached may not address the specific issue that a newborn Christian is struggling to overcome. A new believer might be embarrassed to ask a question in a small group. While small groups and biblical sermons are essential for growth of the body of Christ, "baby believers" need answers to the theological questions they are asking. A team biblical counseling ministry of interactive discipleship offers Christians Christ-centered answers from the Word of God that will satisfy their hunger and thirst for direction.

## Biblical Counseling as Micro-discipleship

*In a biblical counseling session, Pastor Jason was so disappointed to learn that one of the church's most faithful members was caught in the trap of adultery. "How could this have happened?" Jason wondered as he recalled seeing this man attend nearly all of the small group fellowships meetings, Sunday school classes, church programs, and worship services over the past ten years. What Pastor Jason did not know was that this church member would have benefitted from more intimate discipleship in which he could have confessed sins, unclean thoughts, and inappropriate, selfish actions, and received practical instruction from God's Word applied to his life. Though this member's sins were not Pastor Jason's fault, he deeply regretted not starting a biblical counseling ministry as soon as he first saw other church members' need for intimate discipleship years ago. This ministry would have helped Pastor Jason to shepherd the flock of God (1 Peter 5:2).*

The term micro-discipleship[8] has been used to describe what biblical counseling accomplishes. That is to say biblical counseling focuses upon resolving one specific problem area at a time utilizing the Word of God. Christians get "stuck" in their walk with Christ and need a helping hand to pull them out of the mud! Galatians 6:1 states: "**Brothers, if anyone is caught in any transgression, you who are spiritual should restore him in a spirit of gentleness. Keep watch on yourself, lest you too be tempted.**" Helping Christians with serious problems is dangerous work, which is why some church leaders avoid it altogether, but that is unloving to the body of believers. Are you interested in a simple yet profound plan for establishing a safer, stronger, and God-honoring team ministry of biblical counseling and discipleship?

Biblical counseling *is* challenging work, which is why those serving in this type of ministry must have a solid foundation of

[8] Dr. Howard A. Eyrich of the Biblical Counseling Ministry of Briarwood Presbyterian Church, Birmingham, AL, introduced this term to me.

theological beliefs based upon the Word of God. Some programs recommend that those aspiring to be involved in a biblical counseling ministry take over one hundred hours of training. While I applaud the seriousness of this approach, I think there needs to be a healthy balance. We are all called to be ministers of Christ, yet biblical counseling requires skill and maturity; it is a serious call to serve in this manner. Eternal life may be at stake during a biblical counseling session. For this reason and others, a team ministry model is wise.

> **Preach the word; be diligent in season, out of season, reprove, rebuke, exhort with all long-suffering and doctrine. For the time will come when they will not endure sound doctrine but, after their own lusts, shall they heap to themselves teachers, having itching ears; and they shall turn away their ears from the truth** (2 Timothy 4:2-4).

You can be a part of helping Christ's true, universal church make significant changes in the ministry of your local church. As a forgiven sinner, you should be eager to join in the work of the kingdom of God through discipleship, biblical counseling, and personal ministry. Every Christian is called to be a minister according to Ephesians 4:12: **"to equip the saints for the work of ministry, for building up the body of Christ."**

Christ also calls all Christians to fulfill the Great Commission of Matthew 28:18-20: **"And Jesus came and said to them, "All authority in heaven and on earth has been given to me. Go therefore and make disciples of all nations, baptizing them in the name of the Father and of the Son and of the Holy Spirit, teaching them to observe all that I have commanded you. And behold, I am with you always, to the end of the age."** Maybe your current call to "ministry" is informal—to your spouse, children, extended family, church family, or to unbelievers you know as neighbors, co-workers, or friends. Regardless, you are called to obey Christ in these relationships by being an ambassador, or a representative, of Him at all times.

## Is Biblical Counseling Really Discipleship?

In recent years, I have been privileged to serve in a formal capacity of ministry as a "biblical counselor." Someone once asked me: "Isn't it disingenuous of you to equate biblical counseling to discipleship?" By the question, I could ascertain that the person did not consider biblical counseling to be a subset of discipleship, but it is. Biblical counseling is micro-discipleship, meaning that we focus upon one specific problem area at a time in an effort to help the counselee grow in Christ. It takes discipline to change. The counselee must discipline himself to say "no" to the flesh and begin saying "yes" to the Holy Spirit by thinking, speaking, and acting righteously.

Each session provides an opportunity for the counselee to be held accountable for his or her efforts at progressing. If there is a lack of progress, then the counselee must be gently confronted and admonished with the truth in love. Confrontation is not a malicious word! Many act as if it is, but confrontation delivered in love helps us to pause, evaluate our thinking, and determine if our thoughts are in line with the Bible. Here again is the value of the team model. With two counselors, counselees will more likely receive counsel from someone who is similar to them and from someone who is different from them. Biblical counseling is micro-discipleship and team counseling offers the counselee greater amounts of insight. If the counselee is progressing well, then encouragement can be given and other problems can be addressed in a pin-pointed, systematic manner. Again, biblical counseling is a small subset of discipleship.

Most importantly, the heart of the counselee must change. Only God can change the human heart. That is why the Bible is essential in producing heart change. To change, a counselee must hear God's Word of truth. Then, the counselee must begin "doing" His Word of truth. The heart (thinking) and the hands (acting) must be involved for habitual changes to effectively occur.

By "heart," I am not referring to our physical heart that beats and pumps blood in the body. "Heart" is a figurative expression for our inner spiritual person that contains the thoughts, intentions, motives, desires, feelings, and passions that is sensitive to the things of God and is willing and able to receive God's truth. The soul of mankind is what we are pre-eminently concerned with as pastors and biblical counselors. Our physical bodies will die yet our souls will live eternally. God is concerned about renewing our minds (Romans 12:2) which is another way of saying that the heart of mankind must be transformed into the likeness of Christ.

## Strong Believers

While I love evangelism, I equally love strengthening the body of Christ by encouraging disciples to learn to think and act as Jesus did when He walked our planet. I firmly believe that when we invest in the hard work of "soul care" for those who are already saved by grace through faith alone in Jesus Christ (Ephesians 2:8-9), we will be better at evangelizing the lost! Many churches have lost much of their effectiveness and power in American culture today despite abundant availability of both financial and biblical resources. There are more conferences available to Christians on a variety of biblical topics than at any time in history. The Bible can be accessed on the internet and in hotel rooms in America, yet the body of Christ is spiritually anemic. Why?

One reason is a lack of action. Putting God's principles into practice is where exponential growth occurs. Truly, we all need to study sound doctrine and rightly interpret the Holy Scriptures. There is no question about the importance of rightly understanding the intended meaning of God's Word. In addition to Bible knowledge, God calls us to act. However, I find many Christians today are afraid to speak authoritatively about the principles found in God's Word. They are afraid to minister to others for a variety of reasons, many of which are unbiblical and do not please God. We live in a culture of social "correctness" where Christians have been made to believe that it is offensive to share their faith with others. But Jesus said, **"...whoever denies me before men, I will also deny him before my Father who is in heaven"** (Matthew 10:33).

If you can grasp this concept of team ministry presented in the following pages, it just may revolutionize your local church. As you read further, you will specifically learn how you can launch a formal "lay ministry" of team biblical counseling in your church to make disciples by teaching them to observe all that Jesus has commanded them to learn and obey. You can make a difference in your church by doing quality ministry with others. You are not capable of counseling everyone in your church; but in a team setting, you will be able to replicate disciples of Christ as you provide leadership and training in team counseling sessions.

You will learn how to partner with others to conduct the work of ministry specifically called "biblical counseling" and generally called "discipleship." As your partner learns from you, you will learn how to launch them as a mentor to others. Then you can accept another mentoree to learn from you while the person you previously mentored can accept a person to mentor. "Mentorees" soon become mentors in the team approach to ministry. Disciples become "disciplers." Students become teachers. Counselees become counselors. The process of replication is unending in team ministry, and it's all by God's grace.

A balanced, team approach to ministry is necessary for long-term growth of the body of Christ. Team ministry is an excellent way to promote spiritual growth and make disciples of Christ. Team ministry will make you stronger, your mentoree stronger, and the counselees you serve stronger in Christ. It is a win-win-win scenario.

## A Relevant Ministry

*Pastor Jason is so pleased that the church instituted a team biblical counseling ministry. He can now encourage some of the stronger church members to participate in a team ministry that will replicate disciples of Christ and grow his local body of believers more effectively than in the past. The members of Pastor Jason's church are excited, too, because many of them have been aware of the need for a biblical counseling ministry for many years. Now*

*the stronger members of the church have a team-oriented
ministry in which to participate that is effective, and the
struggling members of the church have a viable ministry
within the local church to which they can turn for real
hope and help. It is a win-win-win situation for Pastor
Jason who no longer has to do the work of ministry "solo",
but can train his members to do their part in the body of
Christ.*

There has not been a time in history when a team biblical
counseling ministry has been more necessary and relevant to the
body of Christ. People continue to cry out for answers to a multitude
of problems. The Bible has the answers; however, few Christians
really know how to utilize the Bible to solve their problems. They
do not read, memorize, study, or meditate upon the Word of God.
They do not understand or use biblical words in their daily lives.
They do not think biblically.

Pastors unfortunately have their schedules full of non-
pastoral duties and have very little time left for this intense micro-
discipleship. Even if they do have the time for biblical counseling,
it is usually impossible for one pastor to be this intensely involved
in all the church member's lives. If for some reason the pastor is
unaware of the movement of biblical counseling in the local church,
we who are a part of *Truth In Love Ministries* love to train pastors in
this facet of ministry. And pastors have found that as they improve
their skills in micro-discipleship, their preaching improves, too.

We are committed to training lay persons in biblical counseling,
because the same Holy Spirit resides in their hearts as He does in
the hearts of pastors. The only difference is that many pastors have
spent more time studying the Word of God than a lay person has.
But this should not disqualify a lay person from doing the work
of ministry. A lay person who is growing in Christ and wanting
to help others can do so most effectively in tandem with another
believer. Team ministry is a great vehicle for promoting growth in
Christ.

# Chapter 3

# TEAMS OF TWO

After this the Lord appointed seventy-two others and sent them on ahead of him, <u>two by two</u>, into every town and place where he himself was about to go (Luke 10:1).

Now when they drew near to Jerusalem, to Bethphage and Bethany, at the Mount of Olives, Jesus <u>sent two</u> of his disciples and said to them, "Go into the village in front of you, and immediately as you enter it you will find a colt tied, on which no one has ever sat. Untie it and bring it" (Mark 11:1-2).

And he called the twelve and began to send them out <u>two by two</u>, and gave them authority over the unclean spirits (Mark 6:7).

And he <u>sent two</u> of his disciples and said to them, "Go into the city, and a man carrying a jar of water will meet you. Follow him, and wherever he enters, say to the master of the house, "The Teacher says, 'Where is my guest room, where I may eat the Passover with my disciples?'" (Mark 14:13-14).

It was very recently, and by God's grace, that I stumbled upon this approach we are utilizing in our biblical counseling ministry.[9] It has had a powerful impact on all involved. This team approach to ministry has nearly caused us to delete the words "I", "my", and "mine" from our vocabulary!

---

[9] Our ministry is called *Truth in Love Ministries* and is a non-profit, 501c-3 ministry under the authority of the local church that seeks to replicate and make disciples of Christ globally! Read more about *Truth in Love* in Appendix A.

I am so thankful for men like Dr. Jay E. Adams. His pioneering work in the area of biblical counseling has had far-reaching effects for the kingdom of God. He is a man who had a vision for replication. In the early days of his ministry, he would counsel hurting souls with students observing him at work. Sometimes, he would ask the student to lead the session as he would be there to bail the student out if he got into trouble! Dr. Adams knew the value of counseling in teams for the purpose of replication. Biblical counseling in local churches is now flourishing thanks to the Lord working through Dr. Adams' commitment to training, replicating, and discipling others to do the hard work of biblical counseling.

Another man, the Son of Man, who is also the Son of God, knew the value of teamwork in ministry. As we see in Luke 10:1, Jesus, in His wisdom, sent what we might call "lay ministers" in teams of two ahead of where He Himself was about to go.[10] Likewise, two biblical counselors are sent to meet with an individual, couple, or family where Christ Himself is about to go—Christ will speak through the faithful interpretation of His Word and the illumination of the Holy Spirit.

Mark 6:7 says: **"And he called the twelve and began to send them out two by two, and gave them authority over the unclean spirits."** John MacArthur comments on the biblical history of the two by two concept described in this verse of Scripture with the following:

> This was a prudent practice... employed by Jewish alms collectors, by John the Baptist (Luke 7:19), by Jesus on other occasions... and by the early church... The practice gave the disciples mutual help and encouragement and met the legal requirement for an authentic testimony (Deuteronomy 19:15).[11]

---

[10] Some translations indicate that seventy were sent, however, the point I am emphasizing here is that they were lay leaders sent out in pairs of two.

[11] The MacArthur Study Bible. Word Publishing, 1997.

If you are already involved in a biblical counseling ministry, do you want to improve your effectiveness as a biblical counselor? Do you desire to provide more hope and help to the hurting souls you are privileged to serve? Do you sometimes wish you could replicate more biblical counselors for the purpose of expanding the kingdom of God? Would you like more mutual help and encouragement? Isn't it great when there is another witness (other than you and the counselees) to the wonderful things the Lord does within the walls of a biblical counseling room?

## Pulling Together

Working in teams of two does not mean that the work load is split in half. Rather, when both persons prepare to carry the full load and work together, they find there is surprisingly more power available to them as a team. To illustrate, a friend once told me that a strong horse can usually pull two times its own weight. However, when two horses are harnessed together and pulling together, the weight pulled is not simply doubled as would seem logical, mathematically speaking. Rather, the productivity of two horses pulling together is often six times what they could pull individually!

The strength found in teams of two biblical counselors increases exponentially, too. The two members must be working together in the unity of the Holy Spirit. When they do, the power offered to the counselee is indescribable. On the other hand, if the two team members are not unified in Christ, they will work against each other and accomplish very little. It is similar to a sour marriage in which each spouse pulls against the other by having different goals that are not centered upon Christ. The result is misery for the two in the marriage and all those around them as well.

Likewise in team counseling, two biblical counselors must be unified in their commitment to the sufficiency and authority of God's Word, submitted to the leading of the Holy Spirit, and have the counselees' best spiritual interests at heart, even if that means saying a tough thing to them in a loving way. When unified, two biblical counselors *allow God to do His work through them by the power of the Holy Spirit and His Word*. The Holy Spirit and the Bible provide the mighty power!

## God's Redemptive Power in My Life

In 1995, I completed a thesis for a master's degree in sport psychology. My area of research examined the attitudes of team sport players versus individual sport players. At that time in my life, I was a Christian employed in the secular counseling field and totally unaware that biblical counseling existed. In that thesis, I was interested in studying the mindset of those who are more drawn to team sports than they are to individual sports. Initially, I hypothesized that individual sport players would be more prone to burn out and have a results-oriented mindset.[12] I also hypothesized that team sport players would be less prone to burn out and that they would have more of a process-oriented mindset. In other words, team players would not be as driven by winning as the individual players were. My thinking (based upon the research) was that the context of teamwork would remove winning as the primary focus and result in more value placed on cooperation with teammates.

As with all of psychology's ideas, there were only a couple of marginally helpful ideas that came from that enormously time-consuming study. God's Word, however, offers us far superior truth—Divine Truth. Later in this book, I'll address the findings of that thesis in light of biblical counseling in the local church.

I sometimes lament the fact that I read more about Freud's and Skinner's psychological ideas than I did the pure Word of God during that period of my life. Think how wise I would be if I had studied the Scriptures as intensely as I studied psychological theories. Nevertheless, God had a plan to use that time in my life

---

[12] The term used in psychology is "ego-orientation." This is a secular term referring to someone who is primarily concerned with winning and losing. "Task-orientation" is the opposite term used and refers to being concerned with performing well within the task. These are not biblical terms.

in a redemptive way, and He has now led me into the wonderful world of biblical counseling.

In God's mercy, He has allowed me to start a biblical counseling ministry with a team emphasis designed to replicate disciples of Christ. To my knowledge, there are no other ministries (or even secular counseling agencies) that function the same way that we do at *Truth in Love Ministries*. Nearly everything we do is in teams. We teach, counsel, disciple, and even conduct business (such as interviews) in teams of at least two persons.

The Lord is not limited to one model of ministry as He can accomplish His will in a variety of ways. However, we have found the team approach to biblical counseling through *Truth in Love* to be abundantly beneficial. While other biblical counseling models may be effective and used by the Lord, I believe that the team model for personal ministry is supported by Scripture and powerfully effective for maximum growth in the body of Christ. Not only will counselees grow from a team approach to ministry, but the pair of biblical counselors who work together grow too!

There may be lay people in your local church who have a sincere desire to counsel biblically but who may be concerned about doing it alone. The team approach empowers them to step up and fulfill God's calling. A team approach also provides much more wisdom to the counselee and builds in real accountability. Also, team biblical counselors grow as they learn from each other. During a biblical counseling session, each person can point their partner to a passage in Scripture and teach what that passage means to both the counselee and the other counselor. It encourages people to dig into the Word of God by being students of the Bible. Since we live in an age where so few really know the Scriptures, a team model bolsters a biblical approach by offering the counselee biblical knowledge from two persons.

The apostle Paul had a partner in ministry. He started out with Barnabas as his partner and then later had Silas. Paul was a mentor to Timothy as well. There are other biblical examples of partnerships such as Elijah who mentored Elisha. The "Great Commission" of Matthew 28 is enhanced when two people partner together. Working with a partner in ministry is not a new concept though it has slowly been disappearing.

Admittedly, there are hindrances to the team approach. Cultural influences from psychology impact our thinking and sometimes our unity in ministry. Financial pressures are real and play a big part in the lack of partnerships in many churches today. Pride may also be a factor in the lack of partnerships as people do not know how to work well with others. Poor communication, jealousy, and selfishness may lead to a break in the unity of a team (see Paul and Barnabas). A team of two must work together to be effective, otherwise the team approach fails to reach its full potential.

Overall, however, the united team approach to discipleship in a biblical counseling context has a plethora of benefits. Again, the team approach to ministry offers balance, wisdom, safety, experience, truth, and love. It is a model for ministry that may be utilized in many different contexts. If you are involved in a biblical counseling ministry already, consider how effective you might be if you had a partner pulling with you when you are addressing a difficult situation and challenging counselees.[13] The key is to pull together which means you must be united in Christ. Personal opinions do not always unite us, but God's Word and the Holy Spirit always unite submitted and willing vessels.

---

[13] When I share this team ministry model with NANC members, they get excited about the potential of having two NANC certified persons working together in a biblical counseling session.

# Chapter 4

# NOTHING NEW UNDER THE 'SON'

**What has been is what will be, and what has been done is what will be done, and there is nothing new under the sun"** (Ecclesiastes 1:9).

## Unique but Not New

The team concept is not a new approach to ministry. It's even more than 2000 years old because Jewish discipleship was actually being conducted in the years before Christ's coming. So why do we conduct biblical counseling sessions as individuals now? I think the answer is that the church has a tendency to follow the secular world's framework and goals for psychological counseling. There is also a practical and mathematical aspect of needing twice as many counselors for the task, but as Christians full of the Holy Spirit and God's Word, we should be leading the world in helping people. We are called by God to truly help people, and we don't need to follow the world's framework. Their system is based upon the world's financial concerns and the billing of insurance companies for psychological "treatment." It is not our goal, as the body of Christ to get as many people in and out of the counseling doors as possible. We must be mindful not to model the world but to model Christ.

## The Dangers of Counseling Alone

When you counsel alone, there are some inherent dangers. First, deception is more successful for a counselee when there is only one counselor. Two biblical counselors are better able to prevent, detect, and confront a deceptive counselee during a session. Simply by having two persons involved in the session there is a more serious atmosphere and more protection offered to the biblical counselors.

For example:

> *Sandra is a secular counselor who has been working with a married couple for 8 weeks. Only the husband could come for today's session as the wife was called away to work out of town. During the session, the husband misunderstood one of Sandra's statements and went home and used the statement as "leverage" against his wife. The husband was being manipulative but the wife had no way of contacting Sandra until their next scheduled session in two weeks. In that brief time period, the marriage relationship was strained and the wife considered ending the counseling relationship with Sandra.*

> *In a team biblical counseling model, Sandra and Michael would be paired together to meet with the husband. The husband may still be tempted to be misleading and manipulative but because there are two witnesses, he may think twice. If he is deceptive and twists Sandra's words when telling his wife, at least Sandra has a witness to verify her words and intended meaning at the next session. In Christ's wisdom, He encouraged His disciples to go in teams of two because it provided protection and a second witness.*

A second danger of counseling alone occurs because one counselor often carries a heavier burden. Counselors working in tandem can better fulfill Galatians 6:2: **"Bear one another's burdens, and so fulfill the law of Christ."** Sharing the burden through prayer, Bible reading together, and encouraging discussions is a wonderful blessing of the team model. When a counseling session intensifies, the one counselor who is not directly teaching at that moment should pray for the other counselor who is in the heat of the battle. What a blessing to have a partner who is present praying for you!

A third danger is that one counselor is at a disadvantage in terms of managing the duties of note-taking, Bible referencing, and properly discerning someone's outward/physical appearance, clothing, non-verbal signs. One partner can take notes while the other partner can focus upon listening or speaking. One partner can look up a Scripture reference or watch the counselee's body language while the other is listening or speaking. One biblical counselor may remember the details of a previous session better than the other partner.

Fourth, as mentioned previously, an individual biblical counselor is more susceptible to falling to pride. Counselees admire the wise, individual biblical counselor and esteem him/her to a level of "expert" that mimics the world's methods of counseling. Simply by means of the one-to-one ratio, pride can slip in unnoticed thus stealing the glory of God.

Fifth, everyone is tempted by sin. In a one-on-one model of biblical counseling, there can be temptations by the individual counselor to sin in terms of inappropriate actions or words spoken during the session. Having a partner present brings accountability to the session. For example, a male biblical counselor is encouraged to always have a partner when meeting with a female counselee, even if that partner is a male. Though two males meeting with a female counselee is not ideal, it is better than meeting alone. We must avoid every appearance of evil.

You may have already encountered some of these dangers in your ministry, or witnessed them in the church today. Let's avoid these pitfalls of individual ministry and bring back the old model of ministry by serving the Lord in teams.

## The Church is Plural, Not Singular

When Jesus was in the Garden of Gethsemane praying, He asked Peter specifically to pray and watch with Him, **"And he came to the disciples and found them sleeping. And he said to Peter,**

"So, could you not watch with me one hour? Watch and pray that you may not enter into temptation. The spirit indeed is willing, but the flesh is weak" (Matthew 26:40-41). None of us are as wise or as Spirit-led as Jesus. Like Peter, our spirit may be willing but our flesh is weak. The team dynamic bolsters us; we become more aware of our need to be Holy Spirit-led and a serious-mindedness is brought to the counseling session—both for the counselee and biblical counselors!

A balanced, team approach to ministry better enables us to address sin, and call for repentance. Two persons are better able to listen for unbiblical words or thinking and to lovingly confront counselees with the Word of God so that the counselee does not continue to believe the lies of Satan. In this way, the church body of Jesus Christ is built up as Ephesians 4:11-16 instructs us:

> And he gave the apostles, the prophets, the evangelists, the pastors and teachers, to equip the saints for the work of ministry, for building up the body of Christ, until we all attain to the unity of the faith and of the knowledge of the Son of God, to mature manhood, to the measure of the stature of the fullness of Christ, so that we may no longer be children, tossed to and fro by the waves and carried about by every wind of doctrine, by human cunning, by craftiness in deceitful schemes. Rather, *speaking the truth in love*, we are to grow up in every way into him who is the head, into Christ, from whom the whole body, joined and held together by every joint with which it is equipped, when each part is working properly, makes the body grow so that it builds itself up in love."

While physical church buildings are being erected at an amazing rate, we wonder if spiritual church bodies of Christ are equipped to do the work of the ministry and able to withstand the power of the enemy.[14] Better equipping and better discipleship occurs in team ministry. The church is not a building. The church is the people who gather together in Christ's Name to worship Him, to love and serve each other, and to reach out to those who are lost in the community and world. The church must continue to grow stronger, spiritually speaking, in order to accomplish the goals God has set before it. Team ministry is a powerful tool for churches to build upon the spiritual foundation of Christ.

## Shortage of Mentors

Prior to making the decision to go to seminary, my wife asked me to consider another alternative. She suggested that I ask an older Christian man to meet with me regularly, spend the same amount of hours with me that I would spend sitting in a class, and assign books for me to read. I would pay that man the same amount of money I would spend at seminary. She saw the value of building a real, intimate relationship with a mature Christian man who could mold and mentor me in my walk with Christ. Although I did not follow her plan, the idea has stuck with me because there is such a shortage of mentoring that occurs today, especially in the ministry.

It would have been extremely beneficial for me to follow her advice in addition to going to seminary. Though rigorous, it would have been a great experience. One of the best illustrations of the importance of mentoring came from a blog I read recently about two oxen involved in the hard work of plowing:

> John Bowen writes, "One use of the double yoke was to train young oxen. The farmer would link together an experienced ox and a young ox, and, as they pulled the plow together, the older ox would demonstrate how it was done: the discipline, the patience, the obedience, the stick-to-itiveness".

---

[14] Ephesians 4:12; 4:14.

Picture a young one being yoked to the older. In his youth, he starts by pulling against the master, rebelling, fighting, and ignoring the steady pace of the leader. The older ox walks with purpose, steadfastness, with his eye on the goal. Months later, the younger submits to the other's gait. They plow together, the elder gathering renewed strength from the youth's enthusiasm, fresh approach and eagerness to work. Together, they get the job done. They pace themselves for the days work.

So too, the young Christian is energetic, bold, powerful and eager to work. However, he lacks direction and has the propensity to burn out before a task is completed. For this reason, he needs to be yoked to a mature believer who can help him to learn obedience, humility, loyalty and how to complete the given task, one who will set the pace.[15]

A more mature believer in Christ is like the older ox that "walks with purpose, steadfastness, with his eye on the goal." In the context of biblical counseling, this mature Christian can help a younger, eager biblical counselor to harness his/her energy, boldness, and eagerness by directing him or her toward the right goals. This type of relationship not only helps the counselor, but also all of the counselees who are served through the team model of ministry.

In the Church today, too many Christians, pastors, teachers, evangelists, and lay persons are "isolationists" in ministry. By "isolationists," I mean that they operate more as the Lone Ranger rather than as a team player in a team setting. When an older, more mature Christian takes a young Christian with him to the hospital to visit a sick person, the young person benefits by spending time with the older Christian in a real-life situation and gets to observe real ministry. Eventually, the young Christian will learn how to be a faithful minister like his mentor and discipler.

---

[15] Excerpt from the following internet site: http://convictionofthingsnotseen. blogspot.com/2007/05/illustration-of-ox.html.

The best scenario for younger, inexperienced Christians is for them to observe more mature Christians first. Then, a younger Christian should get an opportunity to be the lead minister with the more mature Christian on hand to assist with any problems or questions. Once the younger Christian is confident (no one is ever perfect or perfectly ready) in personal ministry, he or she should be given a newer Christian to disciple as the more mature Christian breaks away to disciple someone else. This model can be applied to biblical counseling, coaching, discipling, shepherding, and any other form of personal ministry.

## Relationship Dynamics in Discipleship

The team approach is a model of replication. In the Bible, we read of Paul and Barnabas as a team initially (Acts 13:46). Later, a "sharp disagreement" (Acts 15:39) occurred between the two of them resulting in their splitting as a team. Barnabas took Mark with him to do ministry and Paul chose Silas. God is a redemptive God. God is sovereign and allowed this situation to occur, even though sin may have been involved. The redemptive result was that two teams of two were formed for His glory.

Replication and multiplication are essential to the Christian faith and it started with Jesus who concentrated on "speaking the truth in love" to twelve men and to three of them specifically as leaders: Peter, James, and John. The model Jesus chose was not to recruit the multitudes, though He did teach them at times. Rather, Jesus poured His life into a small number of men in a quality way.

In the model of two-by-two ministry, discipleship, spiritual growth, replication, and multiplication occurs. Many people prefer the "Lone Ranger" model to this model for several reasons. For one thing, it takes time and often money to invest in someone else. Have you ever trained someone to perform a task they had never done? It is easier to do it yourself than to train that person because you must carefully observe to ensure that they carried out the task correctly. Sadly, many do not have the patience to train others in ministry.

Some prefer the Lone Ranger approach because they do not wish to allow someone else to see their vulnerabilities in ministry. Every human being has weaknesses; therefore, when two people counsel together, both the senior counselor and the understudy will be able to clearly see some shortcomings and weaknesses in each other. Unfortunately, pride gets in the way of some mentors and teachers who prefer that their trainees never see their flaws. How sad because both the mentor and the student are missing an opportunity to witness the power of God in multiplying and growing disciples for Christ. Humility is a requirement of team ministry.

Ask yourself these questions: Is your ministry about your reputation or the Lord you are serving? Are you willing to be vulnerable to another human being for the purpose of your own spiritual growth? Do you think you must be "perfect" in order to serve the Lord in ministry? Since Jesus Christ was the only perfect person, you must understand that it is pride for you to attempt to present yourself as without sin or weakness. In your weaknesses, Christ is strong and when a counselee is helped despite your weakness, God alone gets the glory. All of ministry is primarily about glorifying God—not ourselves.

A team model of biblical counseling glorifies the Lord better than individual ministry in the following way: two people praying and counseling together are going to convey to the counselee that it is the Lord who does the real counseling by the power of the Holy Spirit. Two people who share the load of teaching de-emphasize the biblical counselor as the "expert." In biblical counseling, we should want to avoid as much as possible anything resembling a secular model of counseling that portrays the human, individual counselor as the expert. We should want to deflect the glory offered to us as counselors to the Wonderful Counselor. God often gets more glory in an effective team approach. God's church that Jesus Himself is building grows more powerful in the "strength in numbers" team approach to biblical counseling and discipleship.

## No "I" in Team

In sports, a common phrase coaches say to their teams is that "there is no 'I' in the word 'team.'" This phrase simply emphasizes to the players that they are playing for the group and not for themselves as individuals. Selfishness is frowned upon in team sports. The goals in the sport are bigger than playing to please one person. The goals are bigger than glorifying one person. Players are not to play for their own glory but for the betterment of the team and for the goal of winning kudos for the school or organization. The team is first and individual play may have to be sacrificed. For example, a great shooter and scorer on a basketball team may be asked to pass the ball to teammates more often so that the team can win, especially if the other team is focused upon stopping the shooter. The shooter will have to trust his teammates.

In Christianity, we are called to lose ourselves in Christ and to put our desires aside for the betterment of the kingdom of God. The goal is winning, though the outcome has already been determined. Christ has already won! In biblical counseling, the goal is to win people into the kingdom of God if they are unbelievers. If the person is already a believer in Christ, then the goal in biblical counseling is discipleship and growth in Christ through obedience to His Word. To achieve this goal, we are called to sacrifice our desires, follow the leading of the Holy Spirit, obey Christ, and demonstrate love to others. A strong partner on the team may be tempted to dominate the biblical counseling session and not allow the weaker partner to speak, but that will not facilitate teamwork. A biblical counselor may seem to go down a different trail during the session, but the Holy Spirit may be leading that way. There are a variety of ways to approach counselees to speak the truth in love to them in most biblical counseling sessions. The focus must be upon pleasing God and helping the counselee in the best possible manner.

# SECTION 2

# THE STRENGTH
# OF
# TEAM MINISTRY

# Chapter 5

# RATIONALE FOR MINISTRY IN PAIRS

**"After this the Lord appointed seventy-two others and sent them on ahead of him, two by two, into every town and place where he himself was about to go. And he said to them, "The harvest is plentiful, but the laborers are few. Therefore pray earnestly to the Lord of the harvest to send out laborers into his harvest. Go your way; behold, I am sending you out as lambs in the midst of wolves"** (Luke 10:1-3).

Notice that Jesus sent out seventy-two others two by two; these were not the Twelve Disciples. In the church today we would refer to them as "lay persons." Verse 2 tells us that Jesus instructed them to **"pray earnestly to the Lord of the harvest"** for more laborers because they were few in number. They were called to a difficult work and were likened to **"lambs in the midst of wolves"** as verse 3 tells us. Their calling and commission to the work of the ministry is not unlike those who are called today to personal ministry like biblical counseling, biblical coaching, biblical discipling, and biblical shepherding.

**Benefits of the Team Model for Counselors**

1. <u>Protection from Traps, Snares and Devouring Wolves</u> We urge all those interested in providing "personal ministry" to those ensnared in sin to have a partner in ministry with them. Jesus gives you the power of the Holy Spirit, but calls you **"lambs in the midst of wolves"**. Biblical counseling is a serious calling to the front lines of ministry. Galatians 6:1 states: **"Brothers, if anyone is caught in any transgression, you who are spiritual should restore him in a spirit of gentleness. Keep watch on yourself, lest you too be tempted."** Notice the warnings throughout Scripture for those doing personal ministry; there are traps, there are snares, and there are devouring wolves.

While Christians do possess the indwelling of the Holy Spirit, they must not think they are immune to falling back on their own strength, according to their flesh. Living by the flesh is easy to do and requires no effort. Living by the desires of the flesh quenches the power of the Holy Spirit in one's life, and can ultimately lead the Christian down a path of destruction and separation from God. The church needs to bring into reality the team approach to ministry to provide protection and accountability to the biblical counselors themselves.

2. A Keener Awareness of the Temptations of the Flesh   There are other protections offered in the team approach. Ephesians 5:7-12 states: **"Therefore do not associate with them; for at one time you were darkness, but now you are light in the Lord. Walk as children of light (for the fruit of light is found in all that is good and right and true), and try to discern what is pleasing to the Lord. Take no part in the unfruitful works of darkness, but instead expose them. For it is shameful even to speak of the things that they do in secret."** Having a partner in ministry helps us to be mindful of our flesh and to reprove evil works of darkness. Some of those seeking counsel may have a sinful tendency toward gossip, or providing unnecessary details of sins[16], or to discuss things deemed by God's Word as unrighteous, unfruitful works of darkness. Christians are called to walk not in the flesh or in darkness anymore, and to take no part in this conversation. We are called to expose these works and words. Another biblical translation uses the word "reprove" them—reprove the unfruitful works of darkness. This can be done so much more effectively with two counselors witnessing the unfruitful speech and reproving it the moment it happens.

3. Protection from False Accusations Having two biblical counselors offers protection from false accusations by a counselee. Some counselees reject the truth in love and in a one-on-one scenario might react by falsely claiming that a counselor used inappropriate words or actions. In a team setting, these accusations are greatly reduced if not eliminated altogether.

---

[16] Ephesians 4:29 and Ephesians 5:4 are other verses that call for us to put away unwholesome or coarse speech.

**Two are better than one, because they have a good reward for their toil. For if they fall, <u>one will lift up his fellow</u>. But woe to him who is alone when he falls and has not another to lift him up! Again, if two lie together, they keep warm, but how can one keep warm alone? And though a man might prevail against one who is alone, two will withstand him—a threefold cord is not quickly broken** (Ecclesiastes 4:9-12).

There is great wisdom in counseling as a tandem rather than in isolation especially in respect to the intimacy that naturally occurs in the counseling context. Deep heart issues are being shared. Again, the accountability of having a partner is a help to ensure that the temptation to sin is minimized thereby decreasing liability, also.

4. <u>Spiritual Growth for the Counselor</u>   When the truth in love is spoken in the counseling context and directed at the counselee, quite often the biblical counselors grow spiritually. One counselor can grow by hearing the other counselor's words from the Scriptures. Of course, the Holy Spirit is essential in all of this growth as He provides the insight by opening the eyes of understanding in the hearts of both counselors and counselees.[17] Do you see the beauty of growing the body of Christ in this way?

5. <u>Training for Lay Persons to Counsel</u>   The team approach for ministry and counseling never suggests pairing two Christians, however committed, to counseling in a formal, official setting without training and experience in accurately handling the Word of Truth. Remember the oxen. The untrained, inexperienced animal was always paired with one who knew what he was doing. Biblical counseling sometimes provokes fear and hesitancy among lay persons, and to some extent, it should. These are real lives and real hurting souls looking for quick solutions and biblical understanding. A lay counselor who is not a lifelong seminary student or Bible scholar might be fearful of giving incorrect

---

[17] Ephesians 1:18.

biblical counsel. Therefore, it is to this person's benefit to have a partner even if the partner is equally new to the concept of biblical counseling.

This hesitancy to counsel alone may prove to be a good thing in one sense as the lay counselor may have a healthy respect for the privilege of speaking into someone's life from the authority of God's Word. The problem surfaces, however, if the lay counselor is too inexperienced and not confident enough in his or her training to provide skilled counseling. Every Christian is competent to counsel another Christian (Romans 15:14) because all Christians possess the indwelling of the Holy Spirit and a copy of God's Word. However, it may take some training, and experience in accurately handling the Word of Truth in a biblical counseling context before the lay counselor becomes proficient in counseling.

## Benefits of the Team Model for Counselees

1. <u>More wisdom and love than one alone can offer</u>   In a medical office a patient may be examined by a doctor who is nearing completion of his or her training and is gaining practical experience through a term of residency.  When your doctor takes over the consultation you may realize you have the wisdom and experience of 2 competent doctors caring for you.

Two biblical counselors working together provide much more wisdom and love than one can offer alone. One counselor may detect a problem area that escapes the other counselor. One counselor may be good at assigning homework while the other struggles in that area of practicality. Recall the discussion in the previous chapter regarding the truth-love continuum. One counselor may be better at speaking the truth while the other counselor may be better at demonstrating love. Herein lies the wisdom of God for co-counseling: the truth can be better spoken in love with two counselors. I reiterate the same point: How important it is to the spiritual growth of the counselee to have the truth spoken to them in love!

2. <u>Married Couples Offer Great Balance and Insight</u>   Often, when a married couple counsels a pre-marital or young married couple experiencing great conflict they can provide great balance and insight to the counselees. The one-flesh married couple can draw on their past walk with Christ to provide hope and practical help for the young couple. If both couples are members of the same church, a married couple of biblical counselors and a newly married couple have the great opportunity to develop a lasting, positive, close knit relationship. A married couple is a product of God's wisdom in making the two "one flesh" and often make a great tandem for team biblical counseling. If you counsel married couples much, think about how many times you might have desired to have your spouse there with you to help you to speak the truth in love.

3. <u>Protection from Potential Harm</u>   A counselee who is getting unbiblical counsel from one counselor may benefit from the other counselor hearing it and correcting it right on the spot. Another way the counselee is protected is from counselors who may be "predatory" in nature meaning they may seek to take advantage of the counselee either financially, sexually, or emotionally. While those types of problems are not frequent in biblical counseling, the temptation that is ever present to take advantage of a counselee is greatly reduced in the format of two by two personal ministry. Accountability is welcomed and encouraged in biblical counseling.

4. <u>Extra Strength for Counseling Devastating Sinful Choices</u> "Extra Strength" is a great marketing phrase for commercial products.  We have access to everything from "Extra Strength" mouthwash to laundry soap and silly glue.  When a counselee is experiencing the devastation and slavery from some sinful choices, two biblical counselors really are better than one.  A pastor and a biblical counselor may work with a young man struggling with a pornography habit, anxiety problem, or depression and find that the help and hope they provide is far superior than what they could offer alone. Maybe two lay counseling men can help disciple a young man in a biblical counseling context by providing great balance and accountability. Since far more people and time resources are necessary when dealing with life-dominating sins,

two biblical counselors are almost prerequisite for many of these difficult scenarios.

5. <u>The Team Approach De-emphasizes the Biblical Counselor as an "Expert"</u>  When two people minister together, the counselee is not as prone to view them as "experts." This benefit surprised us when we first began to do team ministry. We were surprised to find that the counselees were more focused upon Christ and less upon the biblical counselors in a team context. I was concerned that the opposite might occur meaning that the counselee might idolize both counselors, but that has not been the case. The heart of man is prone to elevate a leader to superstar status and one of the most common examples of this is with the preacher. Many Christians think of their pastor who preaches God's Word in a "pope-like" manner which is not accurate.

When two biblical counselors participate equally to bring God's Word to the session, the counselee sees both of them as Christians committed to Christ who is the source of their power. There is nothing special about the two of them. In a biblical counseling situation with only one counselor, the environment tends to lend itself to the idolatrous tendencies in the heart of man. In addition to the protection it offered them, I speculate one reason why Christ sent out His disciples and followers in teams of two is because two ministers pointed people to God the Father rather than to an individual minister. This was real strength in numbers because God received glory, not man.

> *Jacob and Sue are teaming together to help a family dealing with marital conflict as well as a daughter who is tempted by homosexual desires. As they partner together, they recognize that Sue has had personal experience in dealing with a rebellious teenager. Jacob has not had children in his marriage so he is thankful that Sue is in the session. Likewise, Sue is encouraged to have Jacob co-counseling with her because as hard as she tries, she does not think like a man! With their biblical wisdom combined, they are a much stronger team who can point this family to the answers in God's Word through the power of Christ.*

## Two by Two Ministry Fulfills the Great Commandment

It may not seem practical at first, but the "two by two" ministry of Luke 10:1 pays dividends in the long run. Investing in people by training them to become better ambassadors of Christ is a kingdom-focused method that the Lord honors. It is my personal conviction that He will bless and grow His people in a variety of spiritual and physical ways. It may be a step of faith for your church to invest in this type of ministry but the "spiritual return" both here on earth and in heaven will be worth it.

Secular modalities often utilize a model of having one counselor for a group of eight to twenty counselees because it is more cost-effective. Unfortunately, most of them are primarily concerned with the bottom line of making money because secular counseling is big business. However, the biblical model of ministry proposed here elevates the benefits to the recipient counselees above financial matters.

As a biblical counseling ministry, monetary concerns are a reality just as they are in any non-profit ministry, especially one that does not desire to get federal or state funds due to rejecting psychology. Our primary focus is upon worshiping and glorifying God through our ministry. The two by two model of ministry does just that and it serves the counselees well, also, which adheres to the two great commandments in Matthew 22:36-40: **"Teacher, which is the great commandment in the Law?" And he said to him, "You shall love the Lord your God with all your heart and with all your soul and with all your mind. This is the great and first commandment. And a second is like it: You shall love your neighbor as yourself. On these two commandments depend all the Law and the Prophets."** The emphasis in the team approach is upon quality not quantity. Do we want to help lots of people? Yes, but our primary goal is to obey God's command to serve those in a quality way whom the Lord brings across our path.

The counselees' problems are very serious. At *Truth in Love Ministries*, we believe the best way to address those serious problems is by sending two of our trained biblical counselors into that counseling session to do "spiritual heart surgery". Would you go to a surgeon for a heart bypass surgery if he planned on performing the surgery all alone? Of course not! You would want him to have another surgeon present to assist him in the operating room, as well as a team of trained medical support personnel because of the life-threatening nature of the procedure.

Biblical counseling is no different. The hurting souls coming in for counseling require "spiritual" heart surgery offered by trained biblical counselors led by the Holy Spirit utilizing God's Word. If heart change occurs, entire families for generations to come may be saved from a multitude of sins and heartache. Biblical counseling is a vital part of the growth of the body of Christ. We are called to deal with issues affecting this temporary world, while focusing on the eternal consequences. Some of these people may need to hear the Gospel, and two biblical counselors should be better able to discern that spiritual heart condition than just one counselor.

A Christian who dies will have everlasting life. The spiritual heart surgery performed in the counseling room by the Holy Spirit provides long-term health for this life and the eternal life to come. We need to be investing in what really matters: eternal souls. Woe to us if we do not take this call seriously.

# Chapter 6

# Two Extreme Approaches to Ministry

**And he gave the apostles, the prophets, the evangelists, the pastors and teachers, [12] to equip the saints for the work of ministry, for building up the body of Christ, [13] until we all attain to the unity of the faith and of the knowledge of the Son of God, to mature manhood, to the measure of the stature of the fullness of Christ, [14] so that we may no longer be children, tossed to and fro by the waves and carried about by every wind of doctrine, by human cunning, by craftiness in deceitful schemes. [15] Rather, <u>speaking the truth in love</u>, we are to grow up in every way into him who is the head, into Christ, [16] from whom the whole body, joined and held together by every joint with which it is equipped, when each part is working properly, makes the body grow so that it builds itself up in love** (Ephesians 4:11-16, emphasis mine).

If we take a truth of God's Word out of context, or to an extreme, it is heresy and it leads people astray. An effective approach to ministry must be balanced. Disciples of Jesus Christ are eager to share the Good News of the gospel. But the Good News must be balanced with the bad news. Sin is the "bad news" of the Gospel, but understanding this fact is necessary to show us that we all need a Savior for our sins.[18] In the church today, there seems to be two extreme approaches for ministry and neither one is effective. These extremes are love without the truth, and truth without love. For ministry to be effective, these extremes must be combined and balanced. In a sense, the extremes point us to the solution!

---

[18] Let me say that I believe that sin is "Good News" for Christians in the sense that it explains why there is pain, suffering, and death in this world. Sin is never good. Our understanding of sin is only good when we know that we have a Redeemer Who rescues us from the punishment of our sins!

Today, Christians desperately need good spiritual balance for growth. Ephesians 4:15 gives us one biblical perspective of spiritual growth: "**speaking the truth in love, we are to grow up in every way into him who is the head, into Christ**." Quite simply, spiritual growth is becoming more like Jesus Christ in thought, word, and deed. He alone is to be the Christian's model for living because no one else is perfect. But this verse also gives us some very important insight into how we are to emulate Jesus: by speaking the truth in love.

What does that simple phrase mean on a practical level? Answering that question is the primary reason for writing this book. In the context of discipleship, biblical counseling, and personal ministry, this is a key factor. Do not miss the importance of the balance of the ideal found in Ephesians 4:15. A good friend and a very wise man once said to me: "Extreme truth and extreme love are really neither." Let's explore this statement further.

## Extreme #1: Love without Truth

People today are urged to simply love, encourage, and accept others without providing necessary hard-hitting truth. Can we really "love people into the kingdom"? Does that really work? It is sometimes referred to as the "social gospel;" an oversimplified approach to "love" people that is devoid of the biblical truth. Scripture says that God is love[19] so this approach is not without merit. However, "love" without truth will not truly help a Christian in long-term growth. Some will argue that this approach gets people in the door of the church and it certainly can accomplish that goal, but are people really being saved and sanctified if the truth is not presented? Does this "extreme love approach" foster an attitude of "the church only exists to serve me" rather than a "how can I serve God and His Church" attitude? In other words, an extreme love approach may promote selfish attitudes in the body of Christ rather than selfless attitudes of service.

Both the individual Christian and the body of Christ experience exponential growth when receiving the truth in love. People should

---

[19] I John 4:8.

experience a loving environment in the church because God is love. However, people should also come to proper understanding of the truth of the Bible.

The Bible is called "special revelation" because it reveals God's character in words written about Jesus who is the Word made flesh.[20] Without the Bible, people might know there is a Creator God but they would not know that He sent His Son as "Immanuel," or "God with us," to redeem us from this sin-cursed, fallen world. They would know God as a Sovereign Creator but not as a Redeemer and Savior. The Bible helps us to know our sinful condition as fallen human beings (beginning in Genesis 3) as well as to know who our Savior truly is as revealed in the Gospels and other books of the Bible. When Jesus Christ was crucified, the glory of God was fully revealed in His attributes of divine love, justice, grace, mercy, and wisdom.

In Christianity, ministers often unwittingly emphasize love without biblical truth in preaching, teaching, counseling, coaching, and personal ministry. The out of balance approach emphasizing love without truth has produced uneducated Christians who do not know the truth but are very loving toward others! John 8:31-32 states: **So Jesus said to the Jews who had believed in him, "If you abide in my word, you are truly my disciples, and you will know the truth, and the truth will set you free."** Notice that the audience Jesus is addressing consists of believers. There are many believers who do not know the truth of God's Word and therefore are not walking with the Lord in freedom. Rather, these believers are ensnared to the bondage of sin and Satan like the Corinthian believers who gave themselves over to idolatry in 1 Corinthians 10:1-22. The truth has not yet set them free in this life though they do possess the gift of eternal life.

When a Christian is ignorant of God's freeing biblical truths, he is more prone to the temptations of sin—more prone to submit himself as a slave to sin again. There are those who say, "This Christian faith does not work and is certainly not all it is cracked

---

[20] John 1:14.

up to be," leading the person to be an apostate (someone who renounces and leaves the Christian faith). The apostate person may have never been truly born again, but they may also be a Christian who was never truly discipled and taught to observe the Word of God and commands of Jesus.[21] Love without truth does not always produce lasting endurance and perseverance for believers.

> *Freddy is a biblical counselor who really struggles with wanting to be liked by others; he is a men-pleaser. He really wants people to know the same grace, acceptance, and loving mercy of Our Abba Father that he has experienced in his life, and people seem to be really comfortable opening up to Freddy. His heart is right in that he wants to counteract the people in the Christian world who exemplify no grace at all to struggling believers. During a counseling session, a counselee reports to Freddy that he spends about 3 hours on his computer each evening after coming home from work. Freddy is reluctant to speak the truth - that his neglect of his wife is a sin of omission. In other words, the husband is failing to do what is required of him in Ephesians 5. In his mind, Freddy is "loving the husband right where he is" and "waiting on the Lord to show the husband his sins."*

## Extreme #2: Truth without Love

The other extreme approach to ministry is Christians who speak the "truth"[22] without love which often results in despair, fatalism, and hurt for the hearers. Think about it in this manner: if the only half of the Gospel presented to you—that we are all sinners in need of a Savior—without the other half that God Himself sent His Son to be your Savior, you would have been dejected by that half-truth of "supposedly" good news. Knowing the truth that you

[21] Matthew 28:18-20, The Great Commission.

[22] The word "truth" is in quotations because God's Truth IS love. Those who speak "truth" without a loving attitude are often not speaking God's Truth though they call it "truth." God's truth is always loving, even when it hurts our feelings a little. Hebrews 12:5-11 reminds us that God's discipline of us is painful for the moment but is ultimately fruitful for us in the long run.

are lost in your sins without knowing about the love of God as Savior offers you no hope. It is true that you are without hope if you are merely trusting in yourself for salvation, but it is not the whole story. The whole story is unfolded in the Bible—God's plan of loving redemption for His lost people. That is the truth in love for believers in Christ.

There are many knowledgeable Christians today. Technology assists us in easy access to sound preaching and teaching of God's Word. It is a wonderful blessing to know the great and many truths of the Bible, but remember that the Bible warns us in 1 Corinthians 8:1 that "...**knowledge puffs up but love builds up.**" In context, this passage of Scripture is addressing the priority of brotherly love. Paul knew that a brother who was instructed and rebuked in the truth without love would be wounded.[23] This is sin against Christ and the brother we are wounding with the truth.

Another biblical reference warns Christians not to boast in having prophetic powers, knowledge, and faith without love. 1 Corinthians 13:2 states: "**And if I have prophetic powers, and understand all mysteries and all knowledge, and if I have all faith, so as to remove mountains, but have not love, I am nothing.**" Love is essential because God is love[24] and to be an ambassador[25] of God one must represent Him accurately by loving Christ and loving others.[26] Speaking the truth without love is like performing surgery on someone with a cancerous kidney without any anesthesia. The surgery is necessary, but would you want it performed upon you without anesthesia to deaden the pain?

God's truth is love. Christians sometimes forget that "**the Word of God is living and active, sharper than any two-edged sword, piercing to the division of soul and of spirit, of joints and of marrow, and discerning the thoughts and intentions of the**

---

[23] I Corinthians 8:11-12.
[24] I John 4:8.
[25] II Corinthians 5:20.
[26] Matthew 22:37-40.

**heart**."[27] God's truth brings conviction; it is a good thing designed to lead us to repentance which is where we need to be. Ephesians 6:17 tells us that "**the sword of the Spirit, which is the word of God**" is a mighty weapon of spiritual warfare. However, just like any weapon, the warrior who uses this weapon must do so only during spiritual warfare against the enemy and under the control of the Holy Spirit. Carelessly swinging the sword of God at a fellow Christian may injure them severely, maim them, render them powerless, or cost them their life. Unfortunately, some Christian counselors who intend to help only do harm to others when they wield the weapon of the Word of truth devoid of the loving lead of the Holy Spirit.

A biblical example of reproving a brother trapped in sin is the occasion when God sent the prophet Nathan to King David to rebuke his sin with Bathsheba and the murder of her husband, Uriah (2 Samuel 12:1-7). Certainly Nathan needed the wisdom of the Holy Spirit to accomplish this daunting task. Note that Nathan did not charge into the presence of the king making strident accusations. No, he lovingly told David a parable that pictured the sins in an indirect way. Unfortunately, David's pride was so great that at first he failed to identify himself and Nathan had to say, "You are the man!" We can learn from this that we must use a gradual approach when speaking the truth in love to an erring brother or sister.

*Fredricka is a biblical counselor who really struggles with self-righteousness. She wants to tell everyone the truths that have set her—and many others—free by God's grace. In some ways, her heart is right because she wants to help her counselees. However, her delivery of the truth is often condescending as though she has the "right answers" that the counselee needs. At times, Fredricka struggles with being "the god of answers" to her counselees though she would never conceive of it in that way. Her counselees leave her sessions with an elevated view of Fredricka as the "expert" who has all of the biblical answers for them. Sometimes, this causes a problem for counselees who*

---

[27] Hebrews 4:12.

*have become dependent upon Fredricka rather than upon Christ. Some counselees look to her for answers rather than turning to their Savior, Jesus Christ, and the life-giving Word of God.*

## Speaking the Truth in Love in Teams

The team approach to biblical counseling offers more balance in the arena of speaking the truth in love. It is my hope that you can now see more clearly the importance of "**speaking the truth in love**" in the context of a personal ministry such as biblical counseling, coaching, discipling, and shepherding as well as in the context of public ministry like preaching and teaching. Your ministry must be a balanced approach containing both elements of truth and love. In reality, the truth must be presented in love or it ceases to be the truth since God is love. Likewise, real love always contains the truth of God's Word or it ceases to be love since Jesus is "the way, and the _truth_, and the life" according to John 14:6.

A team ministry approach to biblical counseling offers the best opportunity for the truth to be spoken in love to the counselee. When two people are working together as counselors, they tend to be more balanced overall. When two people are partnered together as biblical counselors who humanly tend to err on opposite sides of the truth-love continuum, there is exponential strength as the Holy Spirit uses both persons to minister His truth in love directly applied to the problems of the counselee. And to God be the glory!

Partnering in counseling with a weaker team member can be challenging to your patience. In a team approach, you may be asked to sacrifice your comfort to spend time instructing a partner about a particular aspect of Scripture. You may have to speak the truth in love to your partner in ministry. You may have to practice the very communication and conflict resolution skills that you teach in a counseling session. Your walk with Christ will be challenged but you will grow as a result of meeting the task at hand. The Christian life was never meant to be conducted alone (Ephesians

4:1-3). Though it may be a sacrifice and require more effort, the team approach offers strength in numbers.

> *Freddy and Fredricka are biblical counselors who now partner together in a ministry like Truth in Love Ministries. When they work with married couples, they are at their best. Freddy is able to reflect God's grace and kindness to counselees while Fredricka is able to speak the truth to counselees. At times, Freddy is strengthened by Fredricka's fearlessness since he struggles with men-pleasing and the fear of man. At times, Fredricka is reminded by the Holy Spirit that the souls she is serving are hurting and need the truth spoken in love to them. Without love, Fredricka has learned that she is a "banging gong" and a "clanging cymbal" (1 Corinthians 13:1). The marital counselees that they counsel together now look more to Christ than to either Freddy or Fredricka to be the "expert." They also believe they are loved and receiving honest feedback and truthful counsel from Freddy and Fredricka.*

# SECTION 3

# IMPLEMENTING THE TEAM COUNSELING MODEL

# Chapter 7

## Team Leadership

**Obey your leaders and submit to them, for they are keeping watch over your souls, as those who will have to give an account. Let them do this with joy and not with groaning, for that would be of no advantage to you** (Hebrews 13:17).

You must begin your ministry with the intention of developing leaders. Leaders are not born, they are developed. Some leaders do have God-given abilities to lead that seem "natural" but in most cases, leaders are cultivated like a garden. For leadership skills to develop, persons need opportunities to be followers. Good leaders understand how to submit to other leaders. Before he was king, David understood this better than anyone.

> **And the men of David said to him, "Here is the day of which the LORD said to you, 'Behold, I will give your enemy into your hand, and you shall do to him as it shall seem good to you.'" Then David arose and stealthily cut off a corner of Saul's robe. And afterward David's heart struck him, because he had cut off a corner of Saul's robe. He said to his men, "The LORD forbid that I should do this thing to my lord, the LORD's anointed, to put out my hand against him, seeing he is the LORD's anointed." So David persuaded his men with these words and did not permit them to attack Saul. And Saul rose up and left the cave and went on his way** (1 Samuel 24:4-7).

David had an opportunity to attack and kill King Saul but he understood that God had sovereignly appointed Saul to that position. Even though Saul was seeking to kill David, David knew he could not return evil for evil. David submitted to the Lord rather than taking matters into his own hands.

## Developing Leaders

Good leaders understand who is ultimately responsible for placing a person into a leadership position. God divinely places authority over His people. I encourage the persons who are submitted to my leadership to challenge the *process* but not the *vision* of what we are trying to accomplish. We must be agreed on the vision given to us by God, but the means of carrying out that vision can vary. Good followers who understand their role in the ministry encourage, pray, and speak the truth in love to their leaders in a respectful, submitted manner.

Good leaders need opportunities to lead. While they are followers, they can be given responsibilities to lead small groups or projects in the process of fulfilling the vision. When they succeed in those tasks and leadership roles, they learn. However, when they fail in those tasks and leadership roles, they may learn much more! How someone responds to failure reveals much. As a leader, I give people room to fail. I want them to know they are secure in their position and that failure is part of the Christian life. We all need repentance and forgiveness. Give them opportunities to grow. Push them into a "discomfort zone" to stretch them. They might fail but valuable lessons can be learned for them and for the organization. God is gracious with you so be gracious to those you supervise, disciple, and lead.

Finally, leaders are developed by receiving specific feedback. They need to know what they are doing well and where they can improve. *Truth in Love* staff and volunteers meet in teams to discover and discuss personal strengths and weaknesses. Some people are unaware of their strengths and weaknesses. They need honest evaluations and feedback. To grow, they need to hear the truth in love (Ephesians 4:12-16). God's Word provides an excellent standard to evaluate leaders in ministry. Leaders need time to develop. Bring them along slowly and don't overwhelm them.

## Inflow and Outpouring

It is my belief that all Christians function best in the middle of two relationships: disciple and discipler. Having someone teach and disciple you is important; however, if that is the only relationship you have, then you will become like the Dead Sea, which has no outlet. It has the Jordan River as its source. It is one of the saltiest seas in the world but that saltiness makes it one of the harshest environments for animals and plants to live in; thus, the name "Dead Sea." The problem is that it has no outlet.

Christians will thrive in a relationship with a more mature Christian who disciples him/her (Titus 2:1-6). The key criterion is maturity in Christ which does not always correlate with age. Knowledge of God's Word and obedience to it by the power of the Holy Spirit are the criteria for determining maturity in Christ.

In Matthew 5:13 Jesus said that Christians are to be the "salt of the earth" but He did not mean for them to be a Dead Sea. As a Christian, you need an outlet. You should be discipling others and teaching them what you know. You are to make disciples and to replicate yourself. Too many Christians are always learning and never teaching. Too many Christians are consumed with being "fed" and taught the Word of God, but do not "feed" or teach others.

Husbands should be teaching wives and children. Pastors are to teach their congregations in order to equip them for the work of ministry (Ephesians 4:12). Parents, especially fathers, must be teaching their children (Ephesians 6:4). By the life you live, you are always teaching and influencing others: either for good or for evil! Let us be more intentional in our relationships and teach others about Christ.

## The Team Model for Leadership

Jesus lived with His disciples and knew them intimately. This is where the team model for biblical counseling far exceeds all worldly models. It replicates leaders. By partnering with someone you learn the strengths and weaknesses of your disciple. You can then address those deficiencies with recommendations of books and resources to grow the disciple in those areas. The team relationship affords the leader intimate knowledge and insight that might never be known if the disciple worked alone.

Also, the leader is able to lead by example. Team biblical counseling gives an opportunity for the disciple to learn the passages of Scripture, illustrations, and examples that best address the problem area presented in a counseling session. What a wonderful tool to give a disciple! Rather than just telling the disciple how to handle a situation, the disciple witnesses it first hand. It has blessed me on numerous occasions to see one of my students rightly apply an illustration I used in the past to a new situation. It has blessed me even more to see a student take a counselee to the proper portion of Scripture that speaks perfectly to the problem!

The leader is to be a servant leader like Jesus Christ. Rather than thinking of a worldly model of leadership (dictator-type, power, and control) think in terms of submission and service. Jesus was submitted to the will of the Father (Matthew 26:42). He was a humble servant who came not to be served, but to serve us (Matthew 20:28). As a leader, have a servant mindset toward those among you and the Lord will prosper you and your disciples.[28]

Leaders themselves are strengthened when working with a disciple. I often learn more from a disciple than they learn from me! I may hear a new illustration or be pointed to a passage of Scripture that the disciple would use to address the problem. Disciples are not the only ones who must keep growing: leaders must continue to grow in Christ, too, and that involves being teachable.

*Mary has a Master's degree in biblical counseling from a reputable seminary but she has little practical experience in the counseling room. She is very apprehensive about her*

---

[28] Though not a Christian book, <u>Good to Great</u> by Jim Collins is a helpful book about the humility of servant leadership.

*first team counseling session. Admittedly, she would be more nervous if she were working alone. After the session, she is smiling and excited about biblical counseling. In merely six months of team ministry, Mary has grown to become a leader and a mentor to others in team ministry. Her educational experience now paired with her practical experience in working with a partner has given her confidence. She is so thankful to God for allowing her to grow in Christ.*

## Leaders Begetting Leaders

**So I exhort the elders among you, as a fellow elder and a witness of the sufferings of Christ, as well as a partaker in the glory that is going to be revealed: shepherd the flock of God that is among you, exercising oversight, not under compulsion, but willingly, as God would have you; not for shameful gain, but eagerly; not domineering over those in your charge, but being examples to the flock. And when the chief Shepherd appears, you will receive the unfading crown of glory. Likewise, you who are younger, be subject to the elders. Clothe yourselves, all of you, with humility toward one another, for "God opposes the proud but gives grace to the humble." Humble yourselves, therefore, under the mighty hand of God so that at the proper time he may exalt you** (1 Peter 5:1-6).

So how do you set up this team biblical counseling model in your church? First, you must submit to the leadership of the church. Hopefully, your church has a plurality of elders, deacons, or pastors to whom you can submit. God **"gives grace to the humble"** (1 Peter 5:5) so you must be submitted to the authority the Lord has placed over you. Accountability and responsibility are good concepts. Satan wants us to think that God's authority is not good and that we can trust ourselves, but Proverbs 3:5 says: **"Trust in the LORD with all your heart, and do not lean on your own understanding."**

Now that you are submitted to a local church of human authority as unto the Lord, you are ready to establish your structure for leadership. Initially, you want to have at least one person directly submitted to you. Consider this person to be your partner in ministry. This will be the person into whom you will pour your life in order to replicate yourself.

You must have at least one person who is submitted to you, but you may have up to three persons. The number of persons may depend upon your time constraints and the resources available to you. I would not recommend more than three people. Jesus had twelve disciples yet only three of those were leaders. In Mark 9 and Matthew 17 at the transfiguration, Jesus only took with Him his primary leaders—Peter, James, and John.

In the beginning, I strongly recommend that you only have these two "levels" in your pyramid: your level and those you supervise. As the ministry expands, the levels may increase to three or four levels as the Lord leads. I do not recommend more than four levels in your pyramid. This model will grow quickly once it is unleashed so do not try to speed up the process. Let God develop it in His perfect timing.

## Implementing the Team Counseling Model

Whether you are a pastor, biblical counselor, or a lay person desiring to serve your church congregation more effectively through the personal ministry of biblical counseling, the following section provides a basic structure for you to implement a *team* biblical counseling model. Here is how you can begin the process in your local church.

Since you are the key person with the desire to implement this ministry in your church, you are at the top of the pyramid at the "Supervisor Level," also called Level A. An ideal supervisor has received biblical counseling training with an organization like the National Association of Nouthetic Counselors (NANC) and has experience in biblical counseling. I strongly recommend you receive as much training as possible from organizations like NANC to prepare you to lead others with your knowledge of the Word of God as utilized in a team biblical counseling ministry.

As the Supervisor, remember that you are under the authority of your local church leaders. You must submit to their decisions for your ministry and you must keep them informed of both the good and the bad in your ministry. Underneath your authority, will be 1-3 persons who submit to you as "Leaders in Training," (Level B), who can be elders, deacons, or lay leaders in the church who have spiritual maturity and some interest in mentoring growing Christians. Everyone shall be required to read **Strength in Numbers** to gain understanding of the work involved in discipling, supervising, teaching, and teaming to do the ministry of biblical counseling. Ideally, Level B persons should have some training and knowledge of biblical counseling to prepare them for the work of ministry. If they do not, then plan to meet with them as a small group and teach them the basic principles of biblical counseling in a classroom format.

When both groups of leaders (Levels A and B) are established, you will then begin to do the work of ministry together. Set up a weekly schedule with each of your 1-3 "Leaders in Training" as co-counselors who will partner with you, their "Supervisor." Spend three months working together in your local church. Share resources, biblical insights, and counseling experiences during this period of time. Put together a resource list and purchase some inexpensive booklets to use as homework assignments for counselees. Focus Publishing and other publishers carry excellent resources in small, booklet form to give to counselees. Use these three months to refine your ministry's infrastructure and appointment scheduling process.

After this initial three month period of growing in Christ by God's grace, you and your leadership team are now ready to begin slow expansion. I recommend you offer your entire local church body a 30 hour training class in biblical counseling. You may teach the training course yourself depending upon your experience and knowledge of God's Word as applied to biblical counseling. If you would like one of our *Truth in Love* trainers to assist you, we may be available to schedule teaching and training at your local church. Another excellent option is to contact the NANC office to inquire about their "On the Road Training" courses.

As this 30 hour training class is being taught, you are now developing the third level of the pyramid called "Lay Biblical Counselors in the Church" (Level C). These third level persons should be members of your local church who have completed the basic training course you are offering in biblical counseling. Since the course is made available to the entire church body, you will need to examine those who desire to be involved in this team ministry at your church.

At *Truth in Love Ministries*, we ask prospective Level C counselors to fill out an application, complete a "theology exam," and obtain two recommendations for ministry: one from a pastor of the church and one from a trusted Christian friend. We interview each applicant as well to ascertain their commitment to Christ and implementation of biblical truths in their own lives. The ministry of biblical counseling is serious and often life-threatening in a spiritual sense to the individuals, married couples, and families you will serve. You want to be sure that you prayerfully consider whom you place on Level C: "Lay Biblical Counselors in the Church."

Even if someone is not able to participate in the team biblical counseling ministry in your local church (for whatever reason), many people find the course to be personally valuable. There are many opportunities for Christians to share biblical 'counsel' during informal times with family and friends.

After you complete the examination phase of the process, pair 1-3 persons from Level C with a mentor from Level B of your pyramid. This provides each Level C person with a mentor/discipler and it offers each Level B "Leader in Training" an opportunity to lead and disciple others in Christ. Do not give your B Team leaders more than 3 persons each to supervise. At a maximum you will have three persons on the B Team and nine more persons on the C Team.

That is a total of twelve people and you will find this to be a full schedule to manage.

Preferably, each of these 1-3 "Level C" members will counsel only with each other or with their B Team Leader who is their mentor. You might find it helpful to establish one day per week with 2 slots of team biblical counseling during the late afternoon/ early evening in which all 4 of you can meet together. We call this a "pod" where we offer 4 biblical counselors in a total of 4 biblical counseling sessions (2 sessions going on simultaneously and then 2 more simultaneous sessions follow). Meeting at the same time provides supervision, builds camaraderie, and offers the flexibility of interchanging the 4 biblical counselors if necessary.

Having one evening per week dedicated to this ministry is sufficient to build a solid foundation in your pyramid. In fact, each Level B Team Leader can establish a *different* evening per week to offer late hours. In this way, the burden of offering evening sessions is shared by all involved in the ministry rather than having that burden fall upon one person. This arrangement offers three evenings per week of biblical counseling to those you serve. In the initial stages of development, the Level A Supervisor may want to be more involved. If so, as the Level A Supervisor, you can "float" by alternating evenings each week where you can personally provide an extra partner when unforeseen illness, delays due to traffic, and the like occur.

I strongly recommend keeping the ministry to three levels during your first year and possibly for the ministry's duration. A bigger ministry does not always mean better. Depending upon the size of your church and the number of leaders you are producing by God's grace, the model can be *replicated* which is the bulwark of our ministry. To grow the ministry, you simply *repeat* the process of expansion that occurred for Level C by teaching the same 30 hour introductory biblical counseling course to a new group of people.

If the Lord chooses to bless your ministry, then the word of mouth in your church will plant seeds of excitement in the hearts of God's people because true Christians want to help other people. Examine these persons after they complete the course and then place them into Level C where you may have lost some volunteer biblical counselors.

You may need to move someone up from Level C to Level B, too, to provide more leadership. The same can be accomplished by moving Level B persons up to Level A to help you with the supervision process! I recommend keeping the pyramid small with three simple levels that are replenished from time to time with willing vessels who take the introductory course. Quality in ministry is preferred to quantity as we desire to model Christ.

Another recommendation is that you offer an *advanced* training course in topics like anger, fear, "addiction," depression, heart issues, and a vast array of similar biblical counseling topics. I would offer these classes to challenge your volunteers to keep growing in Christ and in their knowledge of accurately applying God's Word.

Again, please understand that every person in this pyramid structure is counseling others in teams of two. Participants will be paired with a direct supervisor (Level B) in some sessions and with a same-level biblical counseling partner (Level C) in other sessions. In either circumstance, the direct supervisor must oversee each counseling situation by providing knowledge, support and frequent interaction and discussion with those assigned under him/her. These groups of 4 form a "pod" consisting of 1 Level B leader and 3 Level C biblical counselors.

It is preferable to partner the same two persons together for one particular case; however, this may not be possible for *every* session. When you offer 2 slots at the same time, you have more flexibility to allow for people to serve in interchangeable teams of two. When one of the partners on the team is sick or otherwise hindered, it becomes necessary to call in a back-up person to fill the gap. While this is not the ideal situation, at least there is *continuity* because one counselor was present in the previous sessions with that particular counselee. In this system, you minimize canceled sessions due to biblical counselor absence.

In conclusion, do not be too rigid with the pyramid structure that you limit your effectiveness for Christ. The key concept to remember about the pyramid is that everyone in this ministry has someone who is more mature in Christ to disciple them. Each biblical counselor has his/her own ministry outlet as well as a mentor to teach, encourage and shepherd them. Be sure to make the leadership lines clear so that no one ever feels isolated. Supervision is essential in the team model. Accountability is good for everyone. The model presented here is relational and provides care both for those serving as volunteer biblical counselors and for those being served as counselees.

*Jack wants to increase participation in his church's "house to house" counseling ministry—a ministry to those in the church and community who have requested pastoral counseling. He decides to intentionally replicate this outreach by asking Barry, Jim, and Bill to prayerfully consider joining him so that at least one of these men would accompany him on each and every visit. This allows him to mentor each one of them individually as they participate with Jack in team biblical counseling. Jack sees this as an excellent opportunity to train these men for leadership in the church because all three men aspire to be church officers one day. They joyfully accept Jack's offer. Jack arranges for each man to accompany him on the already scheduled home visits, and allows time to return to the church office for discussion of the situations and the biblical principles that apply following each visit.*

*Within six months, Jack observes that two men are more committed to this ministry and have grown substantially in Christ and are ready to help shepherd the flock. The other man is not as committed and his spiritual growth has been slow. This information is helpful for Jack in deciding who to recommend to positions of leadership in the church.*

# Chapter 8

# THE MECHANICS OF ESTABLISHING
# A TEAM MINISTRY

**For God is not a God of confusion but of peace**
(1 Corinthians 14:33).

Previously, I presented a pyramid structure of leadership for replicating biblical counselors by *yourself* in your local church. In this chapter, I want to specify some of the details of how *Truth in Love Ministries* establishes a team biblical counseling ministry in the local churches we serve. My hope is that you will learn from our model of ministry and adapt it to fit your local church. Again, each person involved in your ministry must be submitted to the leadership of the local church. That is non-negotiable. As the Supervisor of the ministry, you must communicate with those leaders because you need their wisdom, accountability, and oversight. Ask at least one key leader to be your contact to meet weekly or at least once every month for prayer and ministry updates. Initially, you will want to meet with this person often in order to solidify your relationship and to build trust.

**Nuts and Bolts**

When you have been approved to do the work of ministry in the local church, start by choosing one day each week to counsel. If you do not have a partner, then ask someone in the church to be your partner during the sessions on that day. If that person cannot commit to a full day, then ask for a half-day commitment from two people. It can be tough for people to carve out a day of their lives to serve in this ministry but do not despair. Stick with the plan to do team ministry. When people get to "taste" it firsthand, they love it!

Ask a staff person at the church to be "on call" in case one of your partners is sick or hindered in some way. An associate pastor or youth pastor is an ideal choice for this responsibility because a senior pastor often has unexpected emergencies such as hospital visits and funerals. Go one step further and consider asking a second staff person to be your second "on call" person. Two are better than one!

Set up your time slots for counseling. We offer 4-5 slots at each location with an hour and a half spacing between each session. That amount of time gives us the flexibility to spend more time in a particular session if necessary. If the extra time is not needed, then it can be used for evaluation and discussion of the past session and future agenda items to be addressed.

## Teaching and Training

*Truth in Love Ministries* desires to fulfill Ephesians 4:12 to equip the saints for the work of ministry.[29] Therefore, a few weeks after we establish the counseling ministry at the local church with which we partner, we begin teaching an on location introductory course to team biblical counseling. We promote the training class to the entire church body with the goal of obtaining lay leaders and lay counselors to serve their church. A mentor or disciple is present at every class, even though he has already completed introductory training. One day soon, this mentor will be teaching the biblical counseling class with one of his mentorees present. Again we are prioritizing the two by two model in every facet of ministry with the goal of multiplication. Nothing is done alone.

Since one course is not enough training, we continue to offer more advanced training while the volunteers work with us. We offer both "theory and the practice" of biblical counseling which can better be known as "theology and practice" of micro-discipleship. We strive to be balanced in every aspect of our ministry.

---

[29] For more about the history and structure of Truth in Love Ministries specifically, read Appendix A.

Lay counselors who have taken the classroom training grow exponentially during their opportunities in team biblical counseling. The National Association of Nouthetic Counselors (NANC) has practiced this system of supervising for years by including in their certification requirements observations of actual biblical counseling sessions as well as the practical supervision underneath a Fellow of the organization. The team approach to ministry multiplication that we are using was built upon this concept.

You may not have persons qualified to teach the courses but do not allow that to discourage you. Teach what you know and have learned (just as 2 Timothy 3:14-15 commands) and utilize the plethora of resources available to you through NANC and similar biblical counseling ministries. Knowledge of God's Word and how to rightly apply it to life is essential and there are excellent resources available today. Further, follow the command of 2 Timothy 2:2 and teach what you know to those who are faithful who will also teach others! True spiritual reproduction! God's Word is so practical, profound, and yet simple, isn't it?

> *Shirley has always been interested in counseling and helping others. She heard about the biblical counseling class offered in her church and signed up. During the ensuing 13 weeks, she learned theology as well as how to practically apply the Scriptures to her life. She is so amazed at how the Lord is using the class that she has recruited two of her friends to attend it the next time it is offered.*
>
> *However, where Shirley really learned biblical truths was in the counseling office with a mentor. The actual "doing" of ministry enabled Shirley to apply biblical principles to the lives of those she served in team ministry. She also learned greatly from an experienced, more mature female believer in Christ who counseled with her. Shirley was thankful for the opportunity to learn the theology of the Bible as well as to practice it. Shirley grew more in Christ during that time period than ever before as a Christian and she had been a Christian for nearly 40 years.*

## Advertising

We have discovered that the best advertising is word of mouth—the voices of recommendation coming from the changed lives. Matthew 9:30-31 tells us how the word of Jesus' miracle of healing the two blind men spread though He admonished them not to tell anyone else (and they disobeyed Him): **"And their eyes were opened. And Jesus sternly warned them, "See that no one knows about it." But they went away and spread his fame through all that district."** If you are truly helping people by the power of the Holy Spirit, you will have no need for paid advertising.

Nevertheless, some churches like to mail out postcards or fliers to make the community aware of their services. It is an outreach ministry in the sense that some people might come to a counseling ministry before they would attend the church worship service. They need both and must be encouraged to attend both.

If you choose to advertise, be sure to present the ministry accurately. This is simply a team biblical counseling ministry of your local church. Avoid psychological words in your flier. Make it attractive and use few words! Our *Truth in Love* brochure was developed by our gifted Chief Technology Officer, Michael Durham, and it is one of the most attractive brochures I have ever seen. I can boast about it because the Lord did it through Michael (Proverbs 27:2; 2 Corinthians 10:17).

## Administration

Administration can be a challenge in this type of ministry, but there are those in the church with this gift. Find them. You must have someone who can take phone calls and make appointments for you. We have a full-time volunteer who fulfills this function quite well, but not everyone is blessed to have a godly father who is retired and available, willing, dedicated, and called to serve in a ministry this way! My dad, Ronny Shaw, is an outstanding blessing to our ministry.

Sometimes, a church secretary will volunteer to help with this duty. Someone who is outgoing and socially adept might volunteer to fill this position. You may consider paying this person a stipend for the service of taking calls and making appointments. You will need a dedicated phone line. A cell phone may be fine temporarily until you get a permanent phone line. You can do this yourself at first but as the ministry grows, you will need a part-time or full-time person. In our ministry, we are blessed to have several full-time administrative volunteers, and we desire to avoid adding responsibilities to the church secretary. We desire to be a blessing to the local church and not a burden.

The administrative person manages the office. This person must understand the importance of what the world calls confidentiality; the Bible calls it gossip. Everyone is tempted to gossip, but this Christian must have a proven track record of avoidance of gossip in all its ugly, disguised forms (insinuations, prayer requests, etc.). The biblical standard against gossip must be in the forefront of this person's mind at all times. This is a crucial admonition for those who do counseling ministry.

We acknowledge this person as our frontline ministry partner with those who first contact our ministry. Any administrative duties can be assigned to this person but the primary duties are to schedule appointments and to take care of our counselees. Phone call reminders are made two days prior to the day of the appointment. Counselees are asked to cancel the appointment at least twenty-four hours in advance. It is important that we are good stewards of the resource of time that the Lord gives us. Once again, you might have guessed that we do this ministry in pairs as well. We have a back up frontline person who is completely adept at our computer scheduling program, for those occasions when our frontline person is out of town, on vacation, or unable to reach the phone. Both numbers are posted at *Truth in Love Ministries* phone lines.

## Assigning Cases

When someone calls, we send or email the forms for them to complete and they are instructed to bring them to the first "orientation" appointment. There they meet one of our staff persons for a short introductory appointment. A staff person takes about thirty minutes to explain what biblical counseling is, our policies, our expectations of the counselee, and some general information about our ministry. Next, we give them a <u>Hope and Help Through Biblical Counseling</u> booklet[30] for them to read at home. This is a homework assignment that is due the first session! The initial "orientation" meeting is important for our ministry to decrease the number of "no shows" and late cancellations that occur most frequently on the first session. This meeting also gives the counselee an opportunity to find our location, meet one of our staff persons, and learn about the goals of biblical counseling. It really decreases the anxiety and fear of the counselees.

Another benefit of this initial short meeting is that the ministry staff has time to read over the P.D.I. (Personal Data Inventory, See Appendix A) in order to determine which team is the best fit to work with the prospective counselees. We can ensure that all signatures and consents are completed properly. An "orientation" appointment is not necessary if you are starting a brand new ministry. However, as your ministry grows (and it will grow), then you will want to consider installing this element into the process.

It is important to obtain signed consent by the counselees you serve. You will want to thoroughly explain your ministry to the prospective counselee BEFORE you offer biblical counseling of any form. Do not be excessively fearful in beginning this type of ministry; fear the Lord, and stay away from psychological words, ideas, and techniques. Strive to be purely biblical in your approach and I believe you will see God's Hand of blessing upon your ministry because He honors those who honor His Word.

---

[30] This booklet and the series of booklets are available from Focus Publishing, 1-800-91focus, www.focuspublishing.com, 502 Third Street NW, Bemidji, MN 56601. <u>Hope and Help Through Biblical Counseling</u> is excellent for preparing the counselees for the first session.

The orientation appointment is our attempt to be very clear about who we are and who we are not. We do NOT want the counselees to think we are psychologists, psychiatrists, licensed professional counselors, or the like. We want them to know that we are simply ministers of the Gospel who desire to speak the truth of God's Word in the love of the Holy Spirit. By God's grace, we desire to provide them with biblical answers to the problems they are struggling to overcome! We have confidence in His Word, which when rightly interpreted and presented in the love of the Holy Spirit, yields powerful fruit in the lives of the hearers and doers of it, especially when the two biblical counselors are "pulling together" in a spirit of unity!

# Chapter 9

# WORKING TOGETHER

**And though a man might prevail against one who is alone, two will withstand him—a threefold cord is not quickly broken** (Ecclesiastes 4:12).

The strength of a rope is determined by the number of cords intertwined and woven together. In the team model of ministry, the **"threefold cord"** that **"is not quickly broken"** consists of the Holy Spirit, who is the Wonderful Counselor, plus two willing, committed, skilled, and biblically-knowledgeable counselors. With those three cords, there is incredible strength to offer counselees hope and practical help that really transforms individual lives and families.

Once you have the leadership infrastructure established, you will want to assign partners in ministry. In a team ministry model, you must be flexible and open to change. You cannot be too rigid. Nevertheless, we have found that consistency with partners is ideal. Biblical counseling is best conducted when partners know each other well. Trust is established between the counselors as they work together on a consistent basis.

It may not always be possible to establish permanent partnerships. One day we had scheduled two male-female teams counseling in separate rooms in the same time slot. A sensitive issue arose before the start of a session and we decided to switch our teams to a female-female team to deal with the sensitive issue. That meant that we had a male-male team in the other slot. We found that both sets of counselees were understanding and appreciated our flexibility to meet the needs of the counselees.

Typically, the following rules guide our thinking in assigning partners. To address sexual issues of individual counselees such as sexual abuse, pornography, and sexual sins, we put teams together in same sex matches. For example, two females would meet with a female regarding the issue of sexual promiscuity.

For marriage issues, we schedule the married couple together with a team of a male and a female. The ideal team is one consisting of married partners, but that is not always possible. We ask the male on the team to _model_ loving leadership by opening with prayer and to take the lead in counseling. Early in the session he is to involve the female biblical counselor in the process by asking her to take part. He might ask her, "Would you like to comment or add anything to what was just said?" In this way, she is shown love, honor, and appreciation in front of the counselees and given an opportunity to provide insights and biblical wisdom.

We ask the female to model submission by respecting her male team member and helping him to lead. If he forgets to pray (Heaven forbid!), she may lovingly and respectfully remind him, "Could we ask the Lord to lead us with a brief word of prayer?" Tone of voice is important and the male counselor should respond lovingly to his team member's request. You can see how two persons are important models for the counselees. Every seemingly "little" word and behavior is subject to scrutiny by the counselees so we must strive to glorify Christ and to be mindful of His honor during this process. More counseling can be done simply through the modeling of Christ-like behavior because our actions speak louder than words.

**Partnership Dynamics**

Teams of same-sex counselors must decide who will lead. At _Truth in Love Ministries_, we encourage our teams to open and close each session with prayer. One counselor may open with prayer and the other may close the session with prayer. We find this to be a good balance for our ministry as the counselees get to hear two different hearts praying in unity. The counselor that opens with prayer often takes the lead in counseling by asking the first question. By leading, we simply mean that one person initiates the process. The Holy Spirit is the leader and must guide all sessions.

Sometimes there is a tendency for the biblical counselors to talk to each other rather than the counselees. While not always negative, the biblical counselors must remember to keep the session about Christ and the counselees. This is not a social time. There is often plenty of time after the counselees leave to talk to each other and to evaluate the session.

Evaluating a session after the counselee has left is a good idea as long as the biblical counselors do not gossip. Discussing the issues that arose during the session or the agenda for future sessions is wise, but talking about the sensational details of a revealed subject matter or those details in a personal, intimate, and slanderous manner is wrong. Evaluating what could have been asked and what was said in an effort to learn and improve as a biblical counselor is the reason for having a short time of evaluation.

In a team setting, we need each other's honest feedback and evaluation. Speaking and hearing the truth in love is required for spiritual growth (Ephesians 4:15-16) of all Christians, counselors included! Focus upon the "beam in your own eye" by discussing what you said incorrectly, failed to say, and what Scriptures now come to mind to use in similar situations. Matthew 7:3 states: **"Why do you see the speck that is in your brother's eye, but do not notice the log that is in your own eye?"** As biblical counselors, we must be especially mindful to look at our own shortcomings so that we may improve our counseling knowledge of God's Word and skills of communication. Ask your partner in ministry to critique you lovingly.

Humility is a key attribute in team ministry. Persons who reject the model of team ministry often do so because they do not desire to humble themselves. Do not allow pride to hinder you from replicating yourself in ministry. If you are fearful that others will know what you do *not* know, then you desire the approval of man more than the approval of God. Galatians 1:10 states: **"For am I now seeking the approval of man, or of God? Or am I trying to please man? If I were still trying to please man, I would not be**

**a servant of Christ."** Once again, your reputation as an "expert" is not the proper goal of a biblical counselor. Your desire must be that God be glorified as the real Divine Expert and that His Word is sufficient and true.

## Different Gifts but the Same Holy Spirit

When we assign partners to a biblical counseling case, ideally we pair two opposites. One person is usually more of the truth-teller, who tends to speak the truth in a way that sometimes fails to come across as loving or compassionate. The other person is usually one who speaks in a "loving" way yet may often omit hard-hitting but necessary truth the counselee needs to hear. As far as it is in our power to do so, we want these two styles represented in each biblical counseling session; we have found it offers balance to the counselees and grows each biblical counselor.

You must assess whether you tend to be a truth-teller who is perceived as unloving or a love-speaker who is perceived as not always forthcoming with the hard truth. Hopefully, you are somewhat balanced, yet I've never met a counselor who did not tend to err more on one side or the other.

I encourage you to work with a partner who thinks differently than you and whose biblical counseling style may be different from yours. If you allow your partner to speak freely during the session, you will definitely be challenged and you will grow. A balanced approach of speaking the truth in love (Ephesians 4:15) is essential for growth in the body of Christ according to the Bible.

The dynamics of team counseling produces sparks when these two opposites are paired in persons who are not very balanced and sanctified in the area of speaking the truth in love. Proverbs 27:17 states: **"Iron sharpens iron, and one man sharpens another."** When iron literally sharpens iron, sparks do fly! That may be the case with your partner, so remember to model good listening skills, give each other the benefit of the doubt, assume the best about your partner's motives (1 Corinthians 13:7), and clarify the meaning behind your words and thoughts when necessary. Ask your partner to clarify his/her thoughts if you think that they may not be expressing them in a balanced manner.

What I have found to be true is this: people found in each of these opposite categories often have loving motives and both often desire to speak the truth. One problem is that neither counselor may be aware of his/her strengths, weaknesses, and tendencies to be an extremist toward either truth without love or love without truth. That is where this model of team ministry excels! It exposes the weaknesses and tendencies toward extremist counseling styles during the actual counseling session and after the session when the counselors discuss the case. Being aware of where we fall short of Christ (our perfect example) is invaluable information for our spiritual growth (sanctification).

Just think how formal ministers and informal lay ministers will benefit from observing someone else who is their opposite do the very same work of ministry! In a biblical counseling session, both counselors have the same goals yet choose different means to achieve the same outcome. With an infinite God, there may be infinite ways to accomplish the goals in biblical counseling. When you observe someone else tackling the same problem yet in a different way, you grow as you obtain a new "tool" for your biblical counseling "toolbox." In future sessions, you will be stronger and better equipped to deal with similar problems.

Working together as opposites is a wonderful blessing. It is akin to the married couple who exclaims, "We are so different!" In God's wisdom, He often joins two people together in marriage who are very different. Not only are they different in gender, but they are often different in their childhood upbringing, life experiences, and approach to problem-solving. For these reasons, married couples who listen and learn from each other progress in their sanctification rapidly. The same is true of team biblical counselors who listen and learn from their partners.

Ultimately, the Holy Spirit is the Great Teacher for both biblical counselors according to 1 Corinthians 12:11-14: **"All these are empowered by one and the same Spirit, who apportions to each one individually as he wills. For just as the body is one and has many members, and all the members of the body, though many, are one body, so it is with Christ. For in one Spirit we were all baptized into one body—Jews or Greeks, slaves or free—and all were made to drink of one Spirit. For the body does not consist of one member but of many."** Though you and your partner may think differently and function differently in the body of Christ, you can be a very powerful team when you yield yourselves unto the Holy Spirit and pull together to glorify Him. You will be amazed at the power available to the two of you when you team together as a threefold cord.

**Team-Fostering Ideas**

> *During one particular counseling session, the counselee was asked to read aloud Psalm 51 about brokenness, repentance, and forgiveness. As the counselee finished reading, his eyes began to light up and his expression changed. He gained hope that Christ would forgive him and empower him to overcome his sin of adultery. The Holy Spirit was working in this man's heart as he said the very Word of God out loud. It had been months since he had read the Bible due to the shame of his sin. At the end of that team session, he prayed to re-commit his life to Christ.*

One technique I use in biblical counseling sessions is to ask the counselee himself to read the Word of God. I want them to read it and speak it out loud for everyone to hear. Sometimes during the first session, that Bible reading is the first time in many weeks (or months!) that he or she has read the Bible. Encourage your counselee to be involved in the process.

Always encourage your partnering counselor to be involved too. Some of the best team sessions and teaching times are similar to popcorn popping! Both counselors make short statements or points concerning the same topic. Often, the counselee interjects short statements, too. The counselors get excited about the Word of God and pop like corn in encouragement with each other. God's Word as revelation should excite us!

During each session, we plan to teach at least one short passage of Scripture pertaining to the counselee's problems. We have gained initial insight into the counselees problem from the data forms they have completed. It is best to have an agenda ahead of time and that agenda is often discussed prior to the session. Prepare yourselves as a team with a short agenda meeting, and a time of prayer together prior to the arrival of the counselee. This is a great way to knit your hearts and purposes together in Christ.

Some teams prefer to have one person teach a passage of Scripture uninterrupted. After the passage is taught, the partner can speak to add an illustration or to bring out a point that may need to be emphasized. Working in teams provides beautiful opportunities to bring God's Word to light for the counselees.

With two persons, a counselee has a greater likelihood of connecting with one of the counselor's teaching and thinking styles, which may enhance insight and understanding of God's Word. With this goal in mind, it is advantageous for the counselee to learn from that person who may have experienced and overcome similar trials in life and applied biblical principles to resolve those problems. The counselee will quickly learn from someone whom they view as similar to them.

The relational element in biblical counseling is an important component of the entire process; God's Word is often spoken in love and received in love when two people "connect". Ultimately, the goal is for the counseling process to terminate because the counselee has learned how to biblically solve problems by searching the Scriptures and obeying Christ.

## Unity at All Costs?

Although the optimal environment in team counseling is for partnering, there are times when unity may not be possible. When a partner says something that is clearly unbiblical, the teaming partner has a duty to lovingly speak the truth in love and rightly interpret the Scriptures. There is only one interpretation of Scripture. Do not allow erroneous statements by either the counselee or the counselor to stand; state the truth of God's Word! Proverbs 28:23 states: **"Whoever rebukes a man will afterward find more favor than he who flatters with his tongue."** Christians should desire a rebuke as from the Lord so that they can think and speak more like Christ and His Word.

As long as the rebuke is stated in a loving manner referencing a correct interpretation of Scripture, a biblical counselor should receive it. No one other than Jesus has ever been perfect so we all have faulty thinking in some areas. How else are we corrected if not rebuked by someone who loves us by speaking the truth of God's Word? 2 Timothy 3:16-17 states: **"All Scripture is breathed out by God and profitable for teaching, for reproof, for correction, and for training in righteousness, that the man of God may be competent, equipped for every good work."** A reproof, or rebuke, sets someone straight who was thinking "crookedly." It may hurt for a moment but will bring healing and righteousness. Humility is required for persons to gain from a rebuke or reproof.

*Charlie and Ron are working together on a case for the sixth consecutive week and are a little frustrated with the lack of progress they are making with their counselee who is struggling to overcome a lust problem involving pornography. During the session, Charlie is more forgiving of the counselee than Ron who strongly believes the counselee needs to be confronted and challenged. The counselee needs both of these men to speak the truth in love to him. Ron prays silently and remembers that he can "be angry, but not sin." As he listens to Charlie share the grace and mercy of God, Ron is reminded of God's grace in his life as well. In fact, Ron is thankful for these few moments when he can collect his thoughts, reflect upon God's mercy to him, and then speak boldly the truth that the counselee desperately must hear.*

*When Charlie finishes, Ron speaks in a firm and challenging way. In God's wisdom, the grace and mercy side of this issue was presented first. Ron recognized this as the plan of God and reminded the counselee of the consequences of separation for sinful choices. Ron also reminded the counselee of the admonitions in God's Word that the **"way of transgressors is hard"** (Proverbs 13:15) and that we are not to walk in sin as we once did (Ephesians 4:17-20). At the end of the session, Charlie and Ron join with the counselee in adapting their plan of action for repentance with new homework assignments. The counselee leaves challenged and encouraged.*

The above scenario was the right way to handle this particular conflict. Ron quickly identified this moment as a providential moment for him to pray, process his thoughts, and then to speak challenging words of truth to the counselee that were complementary to Charlie's approach—not undermining. Working with someone who emphasizes a different attribute of God's character is always a challenge yet it will pay big dividends when you view these as opportunities for everyone's growth. Don't view your team member as an adversary, but communicate in an affirming, supportive manner. Always try to build upon what has been said that reflects the truth of God's Word.

If a comment is made that is blatantly *unbiblical* such as, "God wants you to be happy so do what you feel is right," you must react to that statement by renouncing it and replacing it with biblical truth. You could say the following in a respectful, kind, and firm manner: "While I agree with my colleague that God is concerned about your happiness, I would add that He is most concerned about your holiness. I might differ with my colleague in that you must obey Him and His Word, not your feelings. Feelings can lead us astray. I encourage you to do what is right not what you *feel* is right. The Bible is replete with examples of people who did the right thing despite their feelings (like Shadrach, Meshach, and Abednego; Daniel; David; Moses; and Abraham when asked to sacrifice his son)." After the session, you will need to talk to your counseling partner about their unbiblical statement in an effort to help them to see the principle from God's Word of truth. Your partner may very well see the truth from your statement during the session as that is a much more teachable moment!

## Resolving Conflicts: Modeling Christ

Discernment is needed when a statement is made that may be a different application of the Word of God. Since there are many applications of the one interpretation of Scripture, this can occur quite often. When it happens, gently state your application of Scripture and be sure to say that God's Word can be applied in a variety of ways. Do not say that it can be "interpreted" in a variety of ways but "applied" in a variety of ways. Give the counselee both applications. Be accepting of your partner's application and attempt to connect the two if possible. Do not be afraid to present more than one application because God's principles in the Bible can be applied in an infinite number of ways.

Conflicts may occur between partners in ministry. If they do during a session, the two biblical counselors should resolve it right there. Simply take responsibility for your part in the conflict, confess your sins to each other, and ask for forgiveness. Get past the conflict so that you can deal with the issues of the counselee! This type of problem rarely occurs in our ministry, but it is possible.

If problems occur, view those moments as opportunities to grow in Christ. God is redemptive and can make a failure into a lesson learned for both the biblical counselors and the counselee. Failures are not final with the Father. A problem is an opportunity to model Christ, glorify God, and bring lasting change. Counselors are not perfect but they can model repentance and forgiveness before the counselees to practically demonstrate the Gospel message! Think about it this way: your conflict may be a way to share the Gospel in a real, unforgettable, and meaningful manner!

Three of the best movies I have ever watched were produced by a church. They are "Facing the Giants," "Fireproof," and "Flywheel."[31] The characters in all three of these films portray (model) godliness within the story in an honest way. In a world filled with ungodliness on television and movies, it is refreshing to see people on the big screen who are concerned about the glory of God and how they speak, think, and act. When appropriate, I assign these movies for counselees as homework to watch and then discuss at the next session. People read less and less today so when I find godly movies such as these, I recommend them wholeheartedly.

> *This is only the second time that Bob and June have co-counseled with one another. During this marital counseling session, it becomes apparent that Bob believes that knowledge of the Bible and theological thinking are most important in helping counselees to change. This conflicts somewhat with June's belief that loving the counselee is most important in helping them to change. Without knowing each other very well, Bob and June find it challenging to work together at first but as the session develops, they find unity in the Holy Scriptures.*

> *Bob's Bible references show "tough love" to the counselee while June will add Bible references that point to God's mercy and grace. For example, Bob reminds the counselee that* **"we all have sinned and fallen short of the glory of God"** *(Romans 3:23) and June later (and in a respectful, timely fashion) adds that* **"God shows His love for us in that while we were still sinners, Christ died for us"** *(Romans 5:8). The two of them are NOT competing*

---

[31] Sherwood Baptist Church in Albany, GA, produced these movies along with Provident Films.

*with each other but merely pointing the counselees to different attributes of the infinite character of God.*

*During the session, the Holy Spirit is leading Bob and June. The counselees NEVER think they are competing because Bob and June are not—they are simply complementing each other in a beautiful, humble, and Christ-centered way. They truly are acting as a strong team. Though they do not know each other very well at this point, the two of them DO know Christ and His Word very well and that is what unites them!*

*After three months of working together, Bob and June have grown tremendously. They have benefitted from each other's knowledge of God's Word and view of His character. Both of them know God as loving and just and are learning from each other how to be more balanced in speaking the truth in love to counselees. Both of them now have more illustrations and Bible verses to utilize in other counseling situations that help them to be more balanced in their approach to life. Both of them still tend to lean to one side or the other and that may always be the case, but they are finding that their openness to studying God's Word by the power of the Holy Spirit in a team ministry context has provided them with unexpected opportunities to grow in Christ.*

The team biblical counseling model has its pressures and challenges; however, face those challenges directly and turn them into opportunities for redemption. After all, isn't biblical counseling really about making the Lord look good, not you? At times, your counselees will learn from your actions and interactions as much as from your words of instruction. Use your sinful moments to demonstrate the principles of biblical counseling that you teach. Use your sinful moments to demonstrate in a practical manner the love of Christ through repentance and forgiveness. **"So, whether you eat or drink, or whatever you do, do all to the glory of God."**[32]

---

[32] I Corinthians 10:31.

# Chapter 10

# DOUBLE TEAM

**Only let your manner of life be worthy of the gospel of Christ, so that whether I come and see you or am absent, I may hear of you that you are standing firm in one spirit, with one mind striving side by side for the faith of the gospel, and not frightened in anything by your opponents** (Philippians 1:27-28).

### Shutting Down Your Opponent

In basketball, when one team has an exceptionally talented player, the opposing team's head coach often employs the strategy of a "double team." In this defensive strategy, two players are assigned to guard that exceptional player on the opposite team in order to slow him down. For lay ministry in a biblical counseling and discipleship context, we have found that two are better than one when opposing the lies of Satan, the lies of this world's system, and the passions of our fleshly, sin nature.

Let's be clear about who the opponent really is, however. The counselee is not the opponent. In order for the double team to work effectively, both counselors must know the strategies of the true opponent—the lies of Satan and this world's system—and these lies come in all shapes and sizes. They are too numerous to document in one book. You cannot be aware of all the variety of lies. Knowing the truth of God's Word, will make you better able to detect and confront those lies.

The lies of Satan's counterfeit truth can be compared to U.S. currency. Counterfeit money comes in a variety of forms and bank tellers cannot know every possible counterfeit. They instead concentrate on studying and handling authentic bills and then a counterfeit stands out like a sore thumb. Likewise, the more you handle God's Word by reading, studying, memorizing, and meditating upon it, the more adept you will be at detecting the lies of Satan and this world.

Returning to our double team illustration, one team will have a great advantage when there is inside knowledge of how the opponent prefers to move, dribble, shoot, and pass the basketball. However, if the double teammates do not know *and use* the fundamentals of basketball, they will fail. So, knowledge of the enemy's tactics is not the focus of the double team. Using God's Word in counseling and living out those principles in authenticity between counseling team members or partners is the essential and primary focus in double teaming the enemy. There is great strength in numbers in biblical counseling in the local church!

A licensed professional counselor once said he had terrible experiences with using "lay" counselors in the local church and is hesitant to do it again. On the other hand, I know of very poorly handled experiences that people have had with professional counselors, and I refuse to send people to them if they are not biblically-based. Nevertheless, the solution to the problem of inexperienced "lay" counselors is to have them partnering with more seasoned biblical counselors. We are seeing great growth in the body of Christ as we implement this very concept through *Truth in Love*, where we always minister in teams of at least two.

Once again, the opponent is not the counselee but the lies that he or she believes that do not match God's Word. According to 2 Timothy 3:16, your job in teaming together is to identify those lies according to the Bible, cast those lies down by reproof, correct the lies with the truth of God's Word, and then help the counselee learn how to implement and maintain that new way of living in accordance with God's Word. 2 Timothy 3:16-17 states: **"All Scripture is breathed out by God and profitable for teaching, for reproof, for correction, and for training in righteousness, that the man of God may be competent, equipped for every good work."** Just as the double team slows down the high scorer in basketball, two biblical counseling partners can slow down the enemy's productivity when the power comes from the Holy Spirit working together with God's Word.

God's Word and the Holy Spirit are working together in a *Divine* double team. This double team casts out the lies of Satan and this world better than anything else in this world. As Christians, we are fighting a spiritual battle. **"For we do not wrestle against flesh and blood, but against the rulers, against the authorities, against the cosmic powers over this present darkness, against the spiritual forces of evil in the heavenly places."** (Ephesians 6:12) Prayer and the Word of God are essential elements of this entire process because they will unite you and your partner in one mind. Do not be **"frightened in anything by your opponent"**[33] because God is greater than your defeated foes—Satan and this world's system.

## Unity in Side by Side Teams

There are a variety of combinations in a team biblical counseling ministry. As you and your counseling partner grow in this process, you will not always be mentor and mentoree in the counseling room. The combination of your respective life experiences and spiritual growth will develop into a successful side by side relationship in a team.

In the verse cited above, Paul says about those believers in Philippi: **"that you are standing firm in one spirit, with one mind striving side by side for the faith of the gospel, and not frightened in anything by your opponents."** When two Christians counsel together, they must work at **"maintaining the unity of the Spirit in the bond of peace."**[34] Christians sometimes act as if unity is just something that happens in the church, but that is rarely (if ever!) the case. Unity is hard work because Christians have selfish desires in their flesh. When Christians walk in the Spirit, there is unity. However, when Christians walk according to their flesh, there is great disunity. It is true for any relationship.

While you and your team member or partner may disagree

[33] Philippians 1:28
[34] Ephesians 4:3

about less important aspects of Christian doctrine, be sure you agree on the essentials. The Gospel, eternal life, assurance of salvation, sin, God's Word, and prayer are areas where you need to be in agreement. In a day when there are so many Christian denominations, it is easy to get caught in a sinful snare of division over non-essential (yet important) areas such as baptism and styles of praise music. Be unified in the Spirit having one mind that is focused entirely upon glorifying the Lord Jesus Christ and pointing your counselees to Him. The goal is that the Lord would be gracious to allow the counselee either to connect to Him for the first time or to re-connect to Him as a believer in Christ who was caught in sin.

At *Truth in Love Ministries*, it has been refreshing for me to watch two people team up from different denominations. I usually am aware of each person's stance on a particular doctrine of the faith and where the two will disagree; however, I refrain from pointing this out overtly, and then prayerfully allow the Lord to draw them together in Christ. After they work together for a short time, it becomes apparent to each of them that they are different in some aspects of their faith yet they have established rapport and unity in Christ that supersedes their divisive beliefs on the nonessentials. What a joy it is for me to watch God knit hearts together! That can only be done in Christ Jesus! There really is unity in Christ alone.

## Double Teaming the Desires of the Flesh

Not only will you battle the lies of Satan and this world, but the other opponent you will confront in a biblical counseling session is the fleshly desires of the counselee. Almost always, a counselee has been thinking, speaking, and acting in the flesh—according to their desires and feelings. This is a dangerous way to live as it is warned against in multiple passages of Scripture. Christians are to live according to the principles of God's Word and not according to their feelings, passions, and desires.

You must listen carefully to a counselee's words and reported actions. The counselee's words will reveal what is in their thoughts, or heart. We call this the "heart"—the internal person consisting of the mind and its attitudes, passions, and desires. Luke 6:45 says: **"The good person out of the good treasure of his heart produces good, and the evil person out of his evil treasure produces evil, for out of the abundance of the heart his mouth speaks."** Simply restated, a person's heart attitudes are either aligned with God and His Word producing good fruit or aligned with the desires of self producing evil fruit. Counselees often produce bad fruit in their lives simply because they are living according to their own laws and passions rather than God's Word.

Your mission as a "double team" is to detect those wrong heart attitudes and then to replace them with godly heart attitudes that reflect the love, justice, and wisdom of God. We have found that two biblical counselors do this much better than one, especially in terms of a lay counseling ministry. Let's face it: most people today do not know the Bible and yet strongly desire to help people and serve God. What they do not realize is that the more they study the Holy Scriptures and apply those principles to their lives, the more they will personally grow and be effective in their ministry. It is that simple. *Truth in Love Ministries* is equally concerned with the growth of our biblical counselors as we are our counselees!

In fact, one reason we allow an hour and a half for our counseling sessions is to have time to discuss the case after the counselee(s) leave. We want to spend some time addressing the past session's successes and failures as well as the future agenda. It is essential that both counselors are vulnerable, honest, and critical of themselves first (Matthew 7:3). Then, each counselor may give the other person honest feedback about strengths and weaknesses in content only: do not attack each other's character or motives.

Counselors can discuss why certain questions were asked or omitted. Observations about personal appearance, body language, tone of voice, and facial expressions can be shared, too. Do not turn this time into a gossip session. The purpose of this time is to improve as a biblical counselor and to grow in Christ—not to sin by gossiping! Discuss your thoughts about the agenda you want to address in future sessions. Determine and take note of the lies of Satan that are causing problems for your counselee. Plan your attack of these problems in a specific sequence. All of this discussion can be recorded in writing to assist your memory before your next session.

## Identifying Sin Issues and Heart Attitudes

Two are better than one in terms of being able to identify wrong heart attitudes as compared to what God's Word says about what our attitudes should be. We have found that two persons are better able to utilize Scripture to point the counselees to a practical correction for the wrong heart attitude. The double team of biblical counselors does not present its own advice, but rather declares the very wisdom of God in His Word to the counselee.

> *Joe and Jackie were in a heated session with a fighting couple. Because emotions were high, Jackie shut down and did not truly hear what each person was saying. Thankfully, Joe heard a very unloving comment from the husband to his wife and a very disrespectful comment from the wife to the husband. Joe was able to lovingly confront each person about their hurtful words out of concern for them. The explosiveness of anger in that moment did not deter Joe, and Jackie was grateful that she had a partner in the session who helped her and heard what she did not. In future sessions, Jackie learned to listen better when emotions escalated.*

It is easy to get distracted in a counseling session. When you have one counselor, a distraction may cause the counselor to miss vital information in the form of words spoken or facial expressions. However, when you have two counselors, it is unlikely that both persons will be distracted at the same time. Two counselors are able to stay focused better and to identify words that express unbiblical attitudes.

In summary, can a Christian counsel, teach, warn, instruct, admonish, and encourage in a one-on-one model of ministry? Yes, of course. The team model is simply an incredibly powerful way to do ministry, especially for biblical counseling and discipleship of lay persons. Even for more experienced biblical counselors, the team model is refreshing, less burdensome, and often more effective than an individual model. I urge you to try it. See how it will enhance your skills as a biblical counselor and more importantly, enrich your walk with Christ.

# Chapter 11

## Faith Works

**For as the body apart from the spirit is dead, so also faith apart from works is dead** (James 2:26).

### Discipleship is Hard Work

Whether in a small group, one-on-one, or in a team biblical counseling model, discipling others is hard work. Only by the grace of God can you learn to be patient with others and do the hard work of discipleship. Pray that God will give you the ability to persevere through the difficult times of ministry. Put your faith to work by doing the hard work of ministry. Seek to replicate yourself in those that you are privileged to mentor, disciple, and teach. Do not allow your ministry to get bogged down with circumstances and problems; keep your eyes on Jesus.

Matthew 14:25-33 is a reminder that you must have faith in the Lord Jesus and keep your focus upon glorifying Him in a team counseling ministry.

> **And in the fourth watch of the night he came to them, walking on the sea.** [26] **But when the disciples saw him walking on the sea, they were terrified, and said, "It is a ghost!" and they cried out in fear.** [27] **But immediately Jesus spoke to them, saying, "Take heart; it is I. Do not be afraid."** [28] **And Peter answered him, "Lord, if it is you, command me to come to you on the water."** [29] **He said, "Come." So Peter got out of the boat and walked on the water and came to Jesus.** [30] **But when he saw the wind, he was afraid, and beginning to sink he cried out, "Lord, save me."** [31] **Jesus immediately reached out his hand and took hold of him, saying to him, "O you of little faith, why did you doubt?"** [32] **And when**

**they got into the boat, the wind ceased. [33] And those in the boat worshiped him, saying, 'Truly you are the Son of God.'**

God gives us the grace to fulfill His calling for our lives (Ephesians 2:10). Do not try to do the work of ministry on your own. Ask for the help of others and partner with them for the sake of the Gospel. Each person who has worked with us as a volunteer in a team setting has given me positive feedback regarding the team aspects of our ministry. Some of them have worked alone in counseling in the past and they say that the *Truth in Love Ministries* model is far superior. They report learning more and treasure the fact that they have a partner to help them fulfill the duties of their ministry. The entire load is not on their shoulders; it is shared with a partner. One man said he learned more in three months volunteering with this ministry than in his entire life—over fifty years.

The vast majority of our counselees appreciate the team approach. At first, I was concerned that they might not open up to us in a team. That is no longer a concern to me. People feel loved, valued, and protected. Very few, if any, secular counseling centers or biblical counseling ministries are teaming two biblical counselors together for the benefit of serving the counselees in a more effective, powerful modality.

I want to reemphasize that working in teams of two does not mean that the work load is split in half. Rather, when both persons prepare to carry the full load, they find that there is surprisingly more power available. Remember the horse illustration; when the horses are harnessed and pulling together in unity, the weight pulled is not simply doubled but increases exponentially to six times what they could pull individually!

Likewise, for two Christians united in Christ working together in the team model of biblical counseling, there is more power available and unleashed when the Word of God is coupled with the Holy Spirit. If you employ this model in ministry, by God's grace, you will see that there is amazing strength in numbers.

## Growing Faith

I am so grateful to the Lord for His Hand in my life. I started out my employment as a Christian in secular psychology working in a variety of capacities of counseling. Then God moved me to a place with an integrated model of "Christian" counseling, combining practices of psychology with the Bible. I actually experienced more spiritual unrest and agony (conviction, really) working in the integrated environment than the purely secular one because the secular model was clear—no God allowed—and if I chose to disobey my supervisors in this directive I knew the One I served. The integrated environment was "murky waters" for me since it combined some biblical principles with man-centered principles in direct opposition to the Word of God. No doubt the confusion within my soul at that time was multiplied in those we attempted to counsel.

During those times in my life, I was burned out. I wanted to quit counseling and find something else to do. I was exhausted, confused, and defeated because I saw the harm done to individuals and families in those two arenas of counseling: secular and integrated Christian counseling. Then the Lord demonstrated His sovereignty to me as He divinely intervened in my life. Two men who did not know one another crossed my path; both mentored me, and both encouraged me to read books by Dr. Jay E. Adams. Those two men, Ken Libby and Don Bowen, are now with the Lord and I know I will see them again one day.

The Lord moved me into biblical counseling. Now, instead of being burned out, I am more energized than ever! My wife and friends often encourage me to slow down because I love to do what I do so much that sometimes I forget that there are only 24 hours in a day. What a blessing to serve the Lord in my passion! God is so good.

God is redemptive, too. Remember that secular thesis I wrote during my sport psychology days, mentioned earlier in this book? I was interested in comparing those who are drawn to team sports with those drawn to individual sports. Initially, I hypothesized that individual sport players would be more prone to burn out and that they would have more of a results-oriented mindset.[35] At the time I had no idea that God would bring me one day to compare individual biblical counseling to counseling in teams!

With that application, I fully understand that individuals do burn out more often and more quickly than team biblical counselors. No one can carry the burdens of biblical counseling alone. We need each other. We are made to be inter-dependent upon each other and most importantly upon the Lord Jesus Christ. We are not designed to function on "islands" independently by ourselves.

The Lord has redirected my focus from worldly, temporal things to Godly, eternal things. I am no longer concerned with improving the performance of tennis players or golfers. Instead, I care about speaking the truth in love to people so they can experience the gift of repentance and forgiveness from Almighty God.

In that thesis, I also hypothesized that the context of teamwork would remove the primary focus from the outcome of winning and direct more focus upon cooperation with teammates. Just like the overwhelming majority of psychological research studies, my study's findings could never say conclusively that the hypothesis was true. God's Word is conclusive and absolute. Hopefully, in this short book, you have found plenty of evidence from His Word that this model for biblical counseling is powerful and effective.

---

[35] By way of reminder, the term used in psychology is "ego-orientation." This is a secular term to refer to someone who is primarily concerned with winning and losing. "Task-orientation" is the opposite term used and refers to someone who is being concerned with performing well within the task.

# Chapter 12

# MISSION AND VISION

**For this reason I remind you to fan into flame the gift of God, which is in you through the laying on of my hands, for God gave us a spirit not of fear but of power and love and self-control** (2 Timothy 1:6-7).

## A Big Mission

*Truth in Love Ministries* is a discipleship ministry of reconciliation. We desire to be used by God to reconcile lost, unbelieving people to Christ, the Savior. We desire to be used by God to reconcile Christians back to Him through repentance and faith. We also want to see people reconciled to one another through the power of Christ so that unity, love, and growth of the body of Christ, starting with the local church, will increase for the purpose of expanding the kingdom of God.

That's a big goal for a little ministry with limited funding, but our confidence is not in ourselves; our confidence is in God. We have big goals, dreams, and vision for this ministry and so far, God has exceeded all of them. In the first four months of biblical counseling and training, we trained 27 people in the basics of biblical counseling and watched our ministry grow from 3 to 17 biblical counseling volunteers. We gained six more administrative volunteers in that time period as well.

The primary reason we have grown so rapidly is that we are a replicating ministry. We do everything we can do in teams so that people can get involved, learn, and grow in Christ. Both our counselees and volunteer biblical counselors love the team approach because they feel safe, loved, and valued. Again, it offers more biblical wisdom, more understanding, more love. And it's not a new concept. We even bring our own biblical resources to give the couselees for homework. Most of those resources are booklets and short books that are published by Focus Publishing, publisher of the book you are now reading. We strive to use booklets since we find that most counselees do not prefer to read lengthy books. All this is offered to the counselees free of charge.

## Operating Challenges: Current and Future

Limited funding has prevented us from structuring our organization in a more solidified way. We depend solely upon tax-deductible donations and financial support from local churches. We are truly living by faith in Christ to supply all in this ministry. And He is always faithful.

Our ideal future goal is as follows. We desire to counsel out of the local church five days each week utilizing at least six employed staff counselors working in teams of two. That's a total of three teams. In addition, we would employ a group of at least 3 trained, staff biblical counselors who would travel to a local church. We would set up an "on-location" biblical counseling ministry at that local church for one day each week. Ideally, our group of 3 would be a mix of gender so that we could best meet the needs of our counselees. The one trained biblical counselor not in session would conduct administrative duties such as greeting those coming in for counseling, appointment-making, "orientation" meetings, and the like. In reality, all three biblical counselors must be interchangeable and familiar with all aspects of the ministry, not just counseling.

Three people at the on-site location are ideal. We have in the past functioned with only two but it is more difficult and less conducive to really helping the counselees. Mixing the gender with two men and one woman is best for us since we can have two men meet with another man. Typically, the on-site local church location will have several women available to help us if we have a woman with a sensitive issue coming in for counseling. When that occurs, we simply utilize our female trained staff biblical counselor coupled with a volunteer from the church, provided that person has been recommended by the pastor and approved by the leadership of the church.

After three months of teaching the evening biblical counseling course, we then interview those from the class who are part of the local church body to identify their interest in working in biblical counseling teams. We seek to identify their strengths, weaknesses, preferred group of people to counsel (i.e. children, married couples, singles), and areas of counseling interest (i.e. fear, depression, and "addiction"). Once we identify two students who are ready to help us, we can then break up our staff team of two biblical counselors into 2 teams, so that each team has a mentor staff person with a student trainee.

In this situation, real learning begins. The wisdom of the team model is that the students learn the theology and "theory" behind biblical counseling and then receive an opportunity to apply and "do" biblical counseling under the supervision of a trained person. All the knowledge in the world does no good if the person does not get a chance to apply it! We have witnessed the *Truth In Love* model for ministry strengthen Christians in word and in action.

We continue to teach the biblical counseling class in an advanced manner. In time, as the members of the church become more confident and proficient in their use of God's Word and their skill and abilities at biblical counseling, we start to use the strongest two members as lead biblical counselors. These persons still have access to staff biblical counselors who supervise them, but we give them an opportunity to lead. When we break out the two teams into a staff person coupled with a member of the church, we then have 4 teams with 8 people involved in the ministry. It may only take 6 months to get to this point, by God's grace.

Replication occurs quickly in this model. We want everyone involved in the ministry as biblical counselors to continue as "students of the Word" for life. They should continue to grow in their spiritual walk with Christ, study the Bible especially related to counseling topics, and attend biblical counseling training sessions. Is three months really enough time to learn all there is about biblical counseling? Certainly not, but we believe the most powerful learning for trainee biblical counselors will occur in the counseling sessions with real-life counselees! We have been so greatly encouraged with how our volunteer biblical counselors have grown in this ministry paradigm (not to mention the counselees we have had the privilege to serve!).

As someone who has worked in all three spheres of counseling (secular, integrated or a "mixed" approach, and biblical counseling), this conviction for a pure biblical approach to counseling fuels my passion for missions. I do NOT desire to carry a handful of psychological ideas and theories to foreign lands. My passion for missions is to proclaim the Gospel to all nations and biblical counseling is an effective vehicle for doing so. Instead of helping hurting people with psychological, man-centered ideas, biblical counseling provides a loving context that preaches the Gospel to unbelievers and believers who have strayed from the Gospel. What do lost people really need? A little self-help and a few psychological tools will only provide temporary relief but the Gospel provides power for this life and for the eternal life to come!

I recently read a "Christian" article to a Kenyan pastor. One statement I read lamented the fact that Africans have limited access to the psychological "help" that is so readily available to Americans. The article was oblivious to the fact that many psychological theories are contrary to the Word of God. As soon as I finished reading that one statement, my Kenyan brother exclaimed loudly, "Praise the Lord!" He was glad that psychological theories had limited access to his Kenyan people because he knew they needed to hear the pure Word of the Gospel. He recognized that many psychological messages are confusing, especially under the guise of so-called "Christianized psychology." As Christians, we are not to promote man-centered ideas but to promote Christ-centered, life-giving truths in love. I urge you to evangelize the lost in the world with the Gospel and not the ideas of the world. Biblical counseling provides one method for reaching lost people with truth of God's Word.

## "Glocal" Vision

*Truth in Love Ministries* is concerned with strengthening the body of Christ worldwide. We are a "glocal" ministry meaning we are focused upon both global and local missions.[36] The combination of those two words forms the new word: "glocal." There is an urgency in our spirit to "go and make disciples of all nations" so we also desire to train pastors in foreign countries to do the hard work of micro-discipleship through the team approach to biblical counseling. If you would like to partner with us in sending out missionaries, please contact us.

We are not afraid of errors or mistakes at *Truth In Love* because we believe God is redemptive. Of course we are not sloppy and avoid error as we are able, but God will correct our errors and turn them into "good" for us and our counselees. We utilize lay persons who have had some training in biblical counseling but we bring them along slowly. When you implement this model of team ministry, it might take time to develop but I think you will be pleasantly surprised at how it can flourish rapidly. The time invested by *Truth In Love* in equipping people for team ministry and cultivating relationships in the body of Christ yields plentiful amounts of fruit for the glory of God. We are privileged to serve Christ through this team approach to ministry. We hope you will "team" with us by employing a lay biblical counseling ministry in your local church!

---

[36] I first heard the concept of "glocal" at a Christian & Missionary Alliance denominational meeting.

# Strength in Numbers

# Appendix A

# ABOUT TRUTH IN LOVE MINISTRIES

God's Hand of blessing has been upon *Truth in Love* in its first year of operation. He has done so much with so little that it has truly amazed all of us who are involved. The purpose of this section is to give glory to Our God by telling you about His mighty power, and to provide you with some specifics of our ministry that will aid you in launching this type of ministry in your local church.

*Truth in Love Ministries* is a non-profit, 501(c)3 ministry submitted to the authority of the local church under the direction of a seven-member Board of Directors. Our officers include a President, Chief Executive Officer, Vice President, Chief Financial Officer, Treasurer, Secretary, and Chief Technology Officer. We also have volunteer biblical counselors who donate their time and talents to serve our counselees. We utilize Christians who have had substantial training from quality biblical counseling training centers as well as student interns from a local seminary. We have been blessed to have thirty volunteers form a wonderful team of talented people serving the Lord through *Truth in Love*.

As a non-profit organization, we are able to accept tax-deductible donations. Although we are a separate organization from the local church at which I am the pastor, we have the full support of the leadership there. As of the writing of this book, we are funded by individual donors and churches that provide weekly financial support for our counseling and teaching services. Counselees occasionally give small donations. By God's grace, we do not charge counselees for biblical counseling, and we provide them with all the recommended counseling homework resources free of charge as well. We prefer to trust God to provide us with adequate funds for the resources we give to hurting souls.

We are good stewards. Our expenses are low and we are not extravagant. The leadership desires to direct spending toward helping people and wants our ministry to be defined as a "giving" organization. In the first year, our two full-time staff persons have been and are currently being paid part-time salaries. It has been difficult for both of these men but very rewarding to see God provide in other ways during this period of time.

We are not opposed to applying for grants but we are cautiously examining the possible "strings attached" to those grants, and as of now we are not receiving any grant money. We do not accept insurance money because we reject psychological counseling. Insurance companies only approve payment to licensed professional counselors (L.P.C.'s) in the state of Alabama. If we were to become L.P.C.'s, then we would have two different sets of ethical standards, which would conflict with one another and cause us to choose between the two. Therefore, we desire to remain faithful to the standards of God's Word.

## We Serve Other Local Churches

When invited, we send three persons to a church to set up a biblical counseling ministry. We have a standard of counseling in teams of two. After lay persons in the church have taken three months of *Truth in Love* classroom training, we split our team counselors into two teams by pairing each person with a qualified lay person. We have a theology exam and application forms for the lay counselors to complete before approving them for our ministry. We are currently considering additional measures to assess readiness for ministry.

Ideally, we prefer that all our volunteer biblical counselors obtain certification with a biblical counseling organization like the National Association of Nouthetic Counselors (N.A.N.C.). We currently require thirty hours of class time with one of our *Truth in Love* trainers before a volunteer begins to sit in with a seasoned biblical counselor. The beauty of team ministry is that the lay person then grows exponentially. Sometimes, I wonder if our ministry is designed more for the counselors than the counselees. I only say that because I often see more effort put into the counseling process by the biblical counselors than the counselees we serve. God grows those who invest in studying His Word faithfully.

Our core curriculum closely resembles NANC's core requirements for certification. In a few years, we will apply to become a NANC Certified Training Center. For now, we do offer NANC certification classes through Birmingham Theological Seminary (BTS) where Dr. Howard A. Eyrich, a Fellow in NANC, is eligible to teach for us. BTS is an approved NANC Training Center.

We believe that biblical counseling is spiritual heart surgery requiring two biblical counselors who are the "surgeons." We want those surgeons to be skilled in Bible interpretation and application of the Scriptures in the counseling context. We want those surgeons to have sound theology and understanding of the Holy Scriptures; however, we realize that it is not possible for every lay person to take hours of course work or seminary level courses. Many of those lay persons work regular jobs and sacrifice much to take our course offerings. We require several resources to be read for our introductory course and several more resources to be read for our advanced courses.

At each church we serve, we supply the appointment cards, free biblical resources for counselees and pastoral staff, and professional brochures to give prospective counselees. Churches provide us with weekly financial support. We find that churches that invest in our ministry reap substantial spiritual benefits. Likewise, counselees who invest both their finances and effort in completing homework assignments reap enormous spiritual benefits. It is a pleasure to see God work in the hearts of committed believers.

Overall, we stand in awe at how quickly God has worked in this ministry. Our counselees have grown rapidly. Several unbelievers have been saved and they have led at least 10 others to the Lord themselves! Wow. God is good. Also, our biblical counselors are growing tremendously in their understanding of Scripture. They are becoming stronger Christians and it is having a ripple effect in their churches. By His grace, this ministry continues to blossom. Please pray for us to stay faithful to His vision for this ministry. Please pray for us to seek to please Him in all that we do. We ask for your prayer support and would love to have you partner with us in this ministry of speaking His truth in love.

## PERSONAL DATA INVENTORY

(The information you provide is confidential)

Name _____

Date of Birth _____ Sex _____

Street Address_____

City_____State_____ Zip _____

Home Phone _____ Cell _____

Business Phone_____

Email Address_____

Education: (last year completed) _____

Employer_____

Position _____ #Years _____

Emergency contact person (friend/relative):

Name: _____ Phone_____

## PHYSICAL HEALTH

Rate your health: Excellent  Good  Fair  Poor

List important illnesses, injuries, or disabilities _____

_____

_____

Have you ever used drugs for other than medical purposes? ____

If yes, please explain _____

_____

Do you drink alcoholic beverages? _____

If so, how frequently? _____and how much?_____

Have you ever had a severe emotional upset? _____

If yes, explain _____

_____

Have you ever had suicidal thoughts or attempted suicide? _____
If yes, explain when and circumstances: _____
_____
_____
_____
_____

What medications are you presently taking? _____
_____

## SPIRITUAL HEALTH

What sins (if any) have you / are you struggling to overcome?

**PAST**                                    **PRESENT**

_____
_____
_____
_____

What sins (if any) have others committed against you that you are
now struggling to overcome?

**PAST**                                    **PRESENT**

_____
_____
_____
_____

Denominational preference: _____

Church currently attending: _____ Member? Y or N

Do you believe in God? _____ Do you pray? _____

Would you say you are a Christian? Y or N or Uncertain

Do you believe Satan exists? Y or N or Uncertain    How often do
you read the Bible? Never __ Occasionally __ Often __ Daily __

Explain any recent changes in your religious life _____
_____
_____

What else should we know about you? _____

---

## MARRIAGE & FAMILY RELATIONSHIPS

Marital Status / Circle One:
Single ___ Steady Dating ___ Engaged ___ Married ___
Separated ___ Divorced ___ Widowed ___
Spouse's Name:_____
Birth Date _____
Age _____ Occupation _____
How Long Employed _____Cell: _____
Date of marriage _____Length of dating _____

Give a brief statement of circumstances of meeting and dating ____
_____
_____

Have either of you been previously married? _____
If yes, explain: _____
Date of previous marriages _____
Date marriages ended _____

Information about children:

| Name | Age | Sex | Living? | Grade in school | Step child? |
|------|-----|-----|---------|-----------------|-------------|
|      |     |     | Y or N  |                 | Y or N      |
|      |     |     | Y or N  |                 | Y or N      |
|      |     |     | Y or N  |                 | Y or N      |
|      |     |     | Y or N  |                 | Y or N      |

Describe relationship with your father_____
_____
Describe relationship with your mother _____
_____
Number of siblings _____ Your sibling order _____
Did you live with anyone other than parents (if so, who?) _____
_____

Are your parents living? _____ Do they live locally? _____

What kind of home did you grow up in? (Check any of these that apply)

_____ Traditional (Father, Mother, Children)

_____ Divorced (With whom did you live? ___ Mom;   ___Dad;
Other_____)

_____ Step-family (Which parents remarried? _____;
did you have to live with step-brothers or step-sisters? ___ )

_____ Authoritarian (Father or Mother made all the rules without
discussion. Would not allow other opinions.)

_____ Substance Affected (____ Alcohol; ____ Cocaine;
___Heroin; ___ Marijuana; Other_____)

_____ Religious (___ In name only; ___Strict; ___Hypocritical;
___ Happy Experience)

_____ Affectionate (____ Demonstrated with hugs, kisses, etc.;
___ Affection present but not openly demonstrated)

_____ Perfectionist (Everything had to be done just right to please
___ Mom;   ___ Dad;   ___ Both)

_____ Emotional (Expressed: ___ Crying allowed but controlled;
___ Anger, screaming allowed) (Repressed: ___ Not shown;
___ Parents showed emotion, but not allowed in kids)

_____ Critical (Parent/s remarked only about the negatives. Not
much praise for good things)

_____ Abusive (___ Physically; ___ Emotionally;   ___ Sexually)

_____ Other: _____

# PROBLEM CHECK LIST

| | | | |
|---|---|---|---|
| _____ | Addiction (drunkenness) | _____ | Homosexuality |
| _____ | Anger | _____ | Hurts |
| _____ | Bitterness | _____ | In-laws |
| _____ | Children | _____ | Rebellion |
| _____ | Depression (sadness) | _____ | Religious |
| _____ | Fear | _____ | Sex |
| _____ | Finances | _____ | Sleep |
| _____ | Forgiveness | _____ | Spousal Abuse |
| _____ | Guilt | _____ | Suicidal Thought |
| _____ | Health | _____ | Other: _____ |

Please describe in a nut shell what you believe the problem is _____

_____

_____

_____

_____

Besides coming for discipleship, please describe what else you have tried to do in addressing this/these issues _____

_____

_____

What are your expectations in coming here for discipleship? _____

_____

_____

# More Resources by Mark Shaw

Divine Intervention – Hope and Help for Families of Addicts

The Heart of Addiction – A Biblical Perspective
   The Heart of Addiction Workbook

Hope and Help Booklets

   Hope and Help Through Biblical Counseling
   Hope and Help for Marriage
   Hope and Help for Husbands and Fathers
   Hope and Help for Gambling
   Hope and Help for Video Game, TV & Internet Addiction
   Hope and Help for Self-Injurers and Cutters

All available at Focus Publishing, 1.800.913.6287
www.focuspublishinging.com


In the Greater Birmingham, AL area you can
Reach Mark Shaw at Truth in Love Ministries


Truth in Love Ministries
P.O. Box 367
Clay, AL 35048

205-910-0085
205-910-9221

www.histruthinlove.org
markshaw@histruthinlove.org